Old Testament Parallels

Laws and Stories from the Ancient Near East

by
Victor H. Matthews
and
Don C. Benjamin

PAULIST PRESS
New York/Mahwah, N.J.

Composition and mechanicals: Saija Autrand/Faces Type & Design.

Library of Congress Cataloging-in-Publication Data

Matthews, Victor Harold.
    Old Testament parallels : laws and stories from the ancient Near East / by Victor H. Matthews and Don C. Benjamin.
        p. cm.
    Includes index.
    ISBN 0-8091-3182-X
    1. Bible. O.T.—History of contemporary events—Sources.   2. Bible. O.T.—Antiquities.   3. Middle Eastern literature—Translations into English.   4. Middle East—History—To 622—Sources.   I. Benjamin, Don C.   II. Title.
BS1180.M42   1991
221.9′5—dc20   90-27750
                                                                                              CIP

Published by Paulist Press
997 Macarthur Boulevard
Mahwah, New Jersey 07430

Printed and bound in the
United States of America

Contents

The Books of Samuel and Kings

The Books of Ezra and Nehemiah

The Book of Psalms

The Book of Proverbs

The Books of Job and Ecclesiastes

The Song of Songs

The Book of Daniel

ACKNOWLEDGMENTS

The publisher gratefully acknowledges the use of the following figures: 13, 21, 22, 23, 51, 53, 58, 81, 94, 97, 98, 99, 100, 103, 106, 107, 108, 109, 113, 114, 117, 118, 123, 124 from *Beni Hasan* Part I Archaeological Survey of Egypt, by Percy E. Newberry, copyright © 1893 by Kegan Paul, London, England; figures 5, 6, 9, 19, 52, 74, 83, 122 from *Reading the Old Testament* by Lawrence Boadt, copyright © 1984, by Paulist Press, Mahwah, New Jersey; figures 2, 4, 7, 12, 16, 17, 18, 20, 30, 32, 33, 43, 47, 56, 59, 77, 111, 112, 121 from *The Mythology of All Races* by S.H. Langdon, copyright © 1963 by Marshall Jones, Boston, Massachusetts; figures 1, 71, 72, 116 from *The World of the Bible,* Volume 1, edited by A.S. Van Der Woude, copyright © 1986 by Wm. B. Eerdmans Publishing Company, Grand Rapids, Michigan; figures 8 and 31 from *The Greatness That Was Babylon* by H.W.F. Saggs, copyright © 1962 by Mentor Books, New York; figure 10, "semitic cosmology," from *God's Word to Israel* by J. Jensen, copyright © 1984 by Michael Glazier, Inc., 1935 West Fourth Street, Wilmington, Delaware 19805; reprinted with permission from the publisher; figures 13, 49, 55, 95, 119 from *How To Read the Old Testament* by Etienne Charpentier, copyright © 1981, by John Bowden; reprinted by permission of the Crossroad Publishing Company, New York, NY; figures 3, 29, 39, 42, 44, 45, 68, 76, 85, 86, 87, 102, 120 from *The Art of Warfare in Biblical Lands* by Y. Yadin, copyright © 1963 by Weidenfeld and Nicolson, London; figures 11, 24, 26, 35, 36, 60, 67 from *The Secret of the Hittites* by C. Ceram, copyright © 1975 by Schocken Books, New York, NY; figures 14, 15, 48, 104, 105 from *Art of Ancient Egypt* by K. Michalowski, copyright © 1969 by Harry N. Abrams, Inc., New York, NY; figures 25, 28, 57, 66, 70, 73, 74, 79, 84, 115 from *The History of Israel and Judah in Old Testament Times* by F. Castel, copyright © 1985 by Paulist Press, Mahwah, New Jersey; figures 37 and 47 from *Mari and Karana: Two Old Babylonian Cities* by S. Dalley, copyright © 1984 by Longman, London; figure 38 from *The Struggle of the Nations Egypt, Syria, and Assyria* by G. Maspero, copyright © 1897 by D. Appleton and Company, New York, NY; figure 40 from *The Egyptians* by C. Aldred, copyright © 1963 by Praeger, New York, NY; figures 41 and 62 from the British Museum, Great Russel Street, London; figures 50, 101, 110 from *The World of the Phoenicians* by S. Moscati, copyright © 1968 by George Weidenfeld & Nicolson Limited, London; figures 54, 61, 64, 78 from *Pastoral Nomadism in the Mari Kingdom* by Victor H. Matthews, American Schools of Oriental Research, Alberta, Canada; figures 63, 65 from *New Bible Dictionary,* copyright © 1962 by Baker Book House, reprinted "courtesy of Inter-Varsity Fellowship," United Kingdom; figure 75 from *A History of Israel from Conquest to Exile* by J.J. Davis and J.C. Whitcomb, copyright © 1980 by Baker Book House, Grand Rapids, Michigan; figure 82 from *Ugarit and the Old Testament* by P. Craige, copyright © 1983 by Wm. B. Eerdmans Publishing Company, Grand Rapids, Michigan; figures 88, 89, 90, 91 from *A History of Sumer and Akad* by L.W. King, copyright © 1910, by Chatto & Windus, reprinted in 1968 by Greenwood Press Publishers, New York, NY.

For our parents

E. Harold and Lillie Mae Matthews
Don C. and Edith B. Benjamin

whose love gave us life

Foreword

One of the things that makes studying the history, art, literature, and the religion of ancient civilizations difficult is the huge gap which exists in time and cultural experience between this era and that of the ancients. Reading documents produced by scribes four thousand or more years ago is tough going at best.

Ancient Near Eastern texts are artifacts recovered by archaeologists. Some, like those from the Dead Sea Valley in Israel and the city of Ebla in Syria, dramatically change the way we reconstruct the social world and religious values of the ancient world and of ancient Israel! Establishing the correct connection between related biblical and non-biblical texts is never easy. Simple solutions are generally misleading solutions. Parallels between ancient Near Eastern texts and the Hebrew Bible can be based on their similarities as well as their contrasts. The biblical and non-biblical text might belong to the same genre. For example, *The Enuma Elish Story* and *The Creation of Sky and Earth Story* (Gen 1:1—2:4a) both belong to the genre *creation story*. Likewise, they may not belong to the same genre, but deal with the same topic. For example, both *The Stele of Mesha* and *The Annals of Joram* (2 Kgs 3:1-27) offer an analysis of The War Between Israel and Moab in 830 BCE.

Some of the most important parallels come from the Middle Bronze period (2000–1500 BCE) and the Late Bronze Period (1500–1250 BCE). For The Books of Genesis (Gen 1—11), Psalms and Daniel, there are parallels from Ugarit in Syria whose liturgical literature reflects Late Bronze period ritual and worship. For The Books of Exodus, Leviticus, Numbers and Deuteronomy, there are parallels from Babylon in Iraq, whose legal library from the Middle Bronze period illustrates the judicial systems like the gate-court as well as a wide variety of legal precedents. For The Books of Joshua and Judges, there are parallels from Amarna in Egypt, whose diplomatic communiqués document the unstable social and political conditions in Canaan during the Late Bronze period. For The Books of Samuel-Kings, Chronicles and the prophetic literature before 587 BCE, there are parallels from Mari in Syria, whose government and diplomatic literature illustrates MB social institutions like *covenant, judge* and *prophet.*

A pioneer in providing both ancient Near Eastern texts and artifacts to Western scholars and students was James Henry Breasted (1865–1935). By 1907 he had published five volumes of *Ancient Texts,* which included translations of virtually every document recovered to that time. In 1919 he founded the Oriental Institute at the University of Chicago, whose museum today houses an impressive collection of ancient Near Eastern artifacts. Recently, Burke Long, in conjunction with other members of the Society of Biblical Literature, inaugurated *The Writings from the Ancient World,* which promises to be an exhaustive critical edition of texts from the epoch of Sumer through the age of Alexander the Great.

However, many teachers today still refer their students to James Pritchard's *Ancient Near Eastern Texts Relating to the Old Testament* (Princeton University Press, 1969) as a companion text to the Hebrew Bible or Old Testament. *Ancient Near Eastern Texts* is a fine critical edition, which provides a virtual picture in English of these ancient documents. However, the translations in this volume are so literally true to the original text that beginning students become lost and frustrated. Furthermore, the volume is too large and too expensive for ordinary classroom use, and given the ongoing and exciting discoveries of more and more ancient Near Eastern texts since 1950, Pritchard, even in the third edition, just does not have all the documents teachers want students to read.

In addition to a two-volume paperback set of Pritchard, other affordable, portable supplements have been made available, for example: D. Winton Thomas, *Documents from Old Testament Times* (New York: Harper, 1958); Michael David Coogan, *Stories from Ancient Canaan* (Philadelphia: Westminster, 1978); Barbara C. Sproul, *Primal Myths: creating the world* (San Francisco: Harper & Row, 1979); Joan O'Brien and Wilfred Major, *In the beginning, creation myths from ancient Mesopotamia, Israel and Greece* (Chico CA: Scholars, 1982). J. Maxwell Miller and John H. Hayes in *A History of Ancient Israel and Judah* (Philadelphia: Westminster, 1986) reprint eighteen parallels to historical texts in the Hebrew Bible. Now there is also an illustrated collection of twenty-five creation stories from around the world told in colorful and flowing language by Virginia Hamilton. *In the Beginning* (San Diego: Harcourt, Brace, Jovanovich, 1988) includes one Egyptian, one Mesopotamian and two biblical creation stories. However, none of these volumes is a complete anthology for use with an introductory course on the Hebrew Bible or the Old Testament and some are now out of print. Therefore, students and teachers still need an up-to-date, readable and affordable anthology of ancient Near Eastern texts.

With this experience in mind and the certain knowledge that students were not getting enough from these readings, we have prepared this edition of *Old Testament Parallels*. We have included some commentary and made note of Old Testament references which are paralleled in these texts. We have created in each case a version of the text which is based on our own understanding of its style and meaning. The English vocabulary and idiom emphasizes the relationship between the ancient Near Eastern text and the biblical text, and imitates commonly used patterns of speech. Wherever possible the poetic character of the text is reflected in our version. These are not literal or visual renderings of the original ancient Near Eastern texts, but responsible paraphrases. Harvey Minkoff ("Problems of Translations—Concern for the Text Versus Concern for the Reader" *Bible Review* 4/4 [1988] 34–40) distinguishes reader-centered translations from text-centered translations. *Old Testament Parallels* offers reader-centered translations which convey to the reader the impression of an ancient text. Translations of ancient Near Eastern parallels to the Hebrew Bible produced thus far have been text-centered. They retain so many linguistic and cultural conventions from the original languages that an English reader gets very little sense from the translation.

The line numbers provided for each parallel are those which appear in the critical editions of the texts.

A colleague who will take time from his or her own work to help you with yours is a blessing. There are no ancient Near Eastern parallels for this saying, but there are many modern examples. We have been helped repeatedly by colleagues who looked at drafts of *Old Testament Parallels* and made many valuable suggestions. We want to thank them all, especially Robert J. Miller (Midway College, Midway KY), Mark S. Smith (Yale University), Diana Edelman (Loyola University, Chicago), and George Ramsey (Presbyterian College, Clinton, SC).

It is our hope that students and lay persons will find these paraphrased translations and chronological outlines helpful in their study of the history of the ancient Near East and of the Old Testament.

Victor H. Matthews
Don C. Benjamin

Fig. 1. Egyptian scribes write on papyrus while holding palettes with red and black ink. Their reed pens are carried behind the ear. Scroll cases stand between the scribes. About 2400 B.C.E.

The Book of Genesis

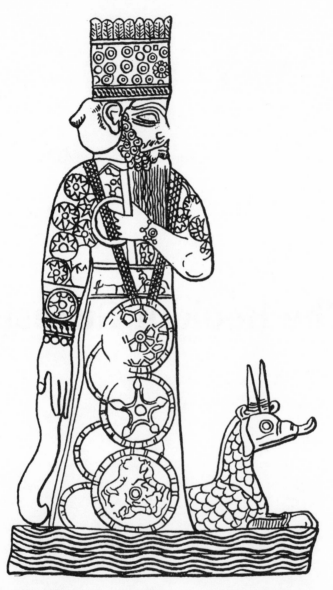

Fig. 2. **Marduk in royal robes with the Mushashu dragon controlling the waters of chaos. 9th century Babylonian cylinder seal.**

The Enuma Elish Story

Between 1792 and 1750 BCE, the empire-building Hammurabi made Babylon the most important city in Mesopotamia and enthroned Marduk, Babylon's patron god, as head of The Divine Assembly. To celebrate these military and political accomplishments, Hammurabi published "The Enuma Elish Story," a revised edition of Mesopotamia's classic story of creation.

In 1849 A.H. Layard, a collector of artifacts for the British Museum, recovered a copy of "The Enuma Elish Story" from Ashur, the Koujunjik, Iraq of today. Ashurbanipal (668–626 BCE) had the copy made for the Assyrian imperial library. It was written on baked clay tablets about thirty inches high in the Akkadian language, using cuneiform script.

Parallels to "The Enuma Elish Story" appear in The Book of Genesis as well as in The Books of Exodus and Psalms (Pss 8, 19, 50, 104). Like "The Enuma Elish Story," these stories and psalms may have been part of the dramatic ritual reenactment of creation at New Years.

Ancient Israel celebrated Yahweh as The Divine Warrior whose armies, commanded by Moses—armed with a staff and The East Wind—confront the armies of the Red Sea, commanded by Pharaoh. Eventually, Israel identified Yahweh, whose name means "The One Who Causes Things to Be" or "The Commander of the Armies of Heaven," as the universal creator as well. Once Israel understood Yahweh both as The Divine Warrior, who liberates Israel from slavery and The Creator of the Universe, the technical cosmological language common in ancient Near Eastern creation stories began to appear in the Hebrew Bible.

(I)

In creation stories, the crisis episode in "The Enuma Elish Story" describes the birth of The Gods of Mesopotamia out of watery chaos through the merging of Apsu, God of Fresh Water, and Tiamat, God of Salt Water (Gen 1:1-2).

When on high . . .
No heaven had been named,
No earth called,
No Anunnaki . . .
There was nothing . . . ,
  nothing but . . .
Old Father Apsu and Mummu-Tiamat, Mother of All Living,
  Two bodies of water becoming one.
No reed hut was erected,
  No marsh land drained,
No Igigi created,
  No names called,
No tasks assigned.
Then . . .
Lahmu and Lahamu were created,
  Their names were called.   *10*
Before they increased in wisdom and stature,
  Anshar and Kishar were created,
  Surpassing their ancestors!
Before they increased in wisdom and in stature,
  Anu was created;
Anu—Kishar's heir—rivaling his ancestors,
  Anu—Anshar's first born—equaling his ancestors!
Anu made Nudimmud-Ea in his image;
  Surpassing his ancestors,
Increasing in wisdom,
  . . . in understanding and in strength.
Greater than Anshar, his ancestor,
  Unmatched among the Igigi, his ancestors. . . .   *20*

Eventually, the increasing noise of the multiplying younger gods disturbed Apsu's rest and he made plans to destroy them— thereby returning the developing order of the universe to its original chaotic state. He was prevented from doing this by The God Ea, who killed Apsu, his father, and took his crown of power. Following

*this aborted crisis, another group of gods were born—among
them, Marduk!*

In the Palace of Fates,
   In the Temple of Destinies,
One Igigi was created,
   The ablest and the wisest of Igigi . . .   *80*
In the Heart of Apsu,
   In the Sacred Heart of Apsu
Marduk was created.
Ea was his father,
   Damkina, his mother.
Divine the womb that bore him;
   Awesome the breasts he nursed.
Marduk's posture was erect,
   His glance inspiring.
His stride commanding,
   His stature venerable.
Father Ea's voice sang,
   His face beamed,
   His heart filled with pride.   *90*
Ea declared Marduk flawless,
   And endowed him with a double share of divinity.
He exalted him above his ancestors,
   Above every last one of them.
Marduk's head was incredible,
   Incomprehensible, inconceivable in power!
No sight escaped his eyes,
   No sound evaded his ears.
His voice was strong—
   His words blazed like fire.
His hearing acute,
   His eyesight sharp.
Marduk's body was unsurpassed.
   His physique was powerful,
His arms and legs were huge,
   His height dwarfed all others!   *100*
"My son,
   My beloved son!
My son, who is my Sun!
   Sun for all the Heavens!"

Clothed with the powers of ten gods,
   Marduk excelled them all. . . .

After an unspecified period of time, Kingu replaces Apsu as Tiamat's companion. He encourages her to destroy The Gods responsible for the death of Apsu. So, she creates monsters to help her defeat The Gods.

. . . she who fashions all things,   *133*
   Gave birth to peerless and hideous monsters.
Serpents with fangs for teeth,
   And venom for blood.
Terrifying dragons,
   Filled with divine power.
To see them is to die,
   Once prepared to strike, they are invincible

Ea and The Gods are afraid to face Tiamat and her allies. At this point, Marduk, God of the Storm and God of Babylon, steps forward to serve as The Divine Warrior for The Gods. For his service, however, he exacts a price.

(III)
If I agree to serve as your avenger and am successful,
   In defeating Tiamat, thereby saving your lives,
The Divine Assembly must proclaim me supreme,
   Let my word, not yours, determine all things.   *120*
What I create shall not change,
   What I command shall not be revoked or altered.

Rejoicing that they have a challenger to Tiamat, The Gods agree.

(IV)
You are the God Most Honored . . . ,
Your word shall not be challenged,
   Your word shall speak for all.
Your decree shall not be altered,
   Your word shall build and tear down
   (Jer 1:10; Eccl 3:3; Matt 16:19)
Your word shall be the law,
   Your command shall be obeyed.

... No God surpasses you!   *10*

. . . .

Marduk is King!   *28*

. . . .

Go and destroy Tiamat,
  Scatter her blood to the winds.   *31*
The Gods approve the mission of Marduk,
  The Ancestors swear allegiance to Bel.

Marduk then arms himself for battle.

Marduk assembles a bow,
  Designs it to his special needs.
Feathers the arrows,
  Ties the string.
Raises his sword,
  Grasps it in his right hand.
Bow and quiver hang at his side,
  Lightning he carries as a shield.
He dons a blazing fire for armor,   *40*
  Weaves a net big enough to trap Tiamat.

*Tiamat, in the guise of a dragon (Ps 74:13–14), taunts Marduk
as he comes onto the field of battle. Taunting before battle was a
common part of military strategy in the ancient Near East (1 Sam
17:8–10; 2 Sam 5:6–8; 1 Kgs 20:1–2; 2 Kgs 18:19–37). Marduk responds to her taunt with a retort. While the taunt itself is a highly
condensed and highly targeted literary form, the retort is even more
demanding. The respondent can only rephrase the taunt by revers-
ing the insult (2 Sam 5:8). New meanings are permitted, new words
are not.*

Fig. 3. **Canaanite sickle sword from Gezer. 14th century B.C.E.**

Why do you raise your hand against The Gods,
    Taking on the air of a queen?
You deceive yourself,
    You cast aside your own children.   *80*
You cannot make Kingu your commander,
    You cannot give Kingu the power of Anu.
You rebel against Anshar,
    You revolt against all The Gods.
Of your armor, I am not afraid,
    Of your monsters, I am not frightened.
I challenge you!
    Come forward alone!
    Duel with me, one on one!
    (1 Sam 17:8-10; 2 Sam 2:18-23)

When Tiamat hears this challenge, she becomes infuriated. Out of her mind with anger, she rushes away from her bodyguard and attacks Marduk by herself.

As she opens her mouth to roar, Marduk inflates her with The Storm Winds making her completely incapacitated. Then, Marduk pierces her heart with an arrow of lightning. Marduk stands triumphant on her dying body (2 Sam 8:2).

The denouement first describes Marduk as The Divine Warrior processing triumphantly to The Sacred Mountain to be proclaimed The King. Here he builds The Holy City. Outside the gate of The City, Marduk erects Tiamat's monsters as statues to remind all who enter of his great victory!

(V)

Marduk rounded up the monsters of Tiamat,   *71*
    Brought them as trophies before The Divine Assembly.
Marduk trapped The Eleven of Tiamat in his net,
    Shattered their weapons,
    Shackled their feet.
Marduk turned them into statues,
    Mounted them at The Gate of Apsu.
"Let these statues be a memorial," he proclaimed,
    "So that this revolt may never be forgotten!"

Having remodeled his own temple with the spoils of war, Marduk then uses Tiamat's body to build The New World. He crushes her skull with his club, and scatters her blood into the wind. He

Fig. 4. **Combat between Marduk and a dragon. From a cylinder seal.**

splits her body in two. He uses half to make The Sky, half to make The Earth and seals out The Waters of Apsu with The Horizons (Gen 1:6–7).

Marduk placed The Gods into The Sky as constellations, three to mark each season of the year. He assigns The Moon to guard The Night and to mark the month with its phases (Gen 1:15–16).

Finally, Marduk and Ea discuss a plan to create humans.

(VI)

I will knead blood and bone into A Savage,
    Aborigine will be its name.   5
The Aborigines will do The Gods' work,
    The Savages will set The Gods free.

Ea suggests that Marduk use one of Tiamat's allies as the raw material for The Savage. So, Marduk convenes The Divine Assembly to discuss Ea's proposal.

Who planned Tiamat's uprising?
    Who advised her to rebel?   23
Hand over the instigator of this revolt,
    Punish the conspirator for his crimes!
    . . . and you shall live in peace.

Fig. 5. **The tower of Babel built by a god. Cylinder seal, 13th century B.C.E.**

The Gods testified:
Kingu planned the uprising!
   Kingu advised Tiamat to rebel!   *30*

   So The Gods bind Kingu and Ea slits his throat. They use his blood to fashion The Aborigines (Gen 1:26–27; 2:7–15), whom Ea assigns to do The Gods' work in The New World.

Marduk arrested Kingu, his rival;
   Ea arraigned him.
Marduk convicted him of conspiracy;
   Ea executed him by cutting his throat.
Ea formed The Aborigines from Kingu's blood,
   Marduk set The Aborigines to work.
Ea emancipated The Gods,
   The Wise created The Aborigines.
Marduk put The Aborigines to work,
   And set The Gods free.
What an incredible accomplishment—
Nudimmud-Ea created;
   Marduk masterfully designed.
Ea the Wise created The Aborigines,
   Marduk ordered them to do The Gods' work.
What an incomprehensible task,
   What a work of art!

The Aborigine designed by Marduk,
  The Savage executed by Nudimmud.
Marduk the King split the Anunnaki into groups,   *40*
  Appointed Anu their supervisor.
Stationed three hundred Anunnaki in the heavens above,
  Three hundred more on the earth below.

To celebrate Marduk's coronation, The Gods build The Esagila, the city of Babylon, where they transfer all their divine titles to Marduk and decree The Akitu, an annual celebration of Marduk as The Divine Warrior at which "The Enuma Elish Story" *is to be retold.*

Fig. 6. **An artist's reconstruction of the ziggurat of Ur, as it may have appeared about 2100 B.C.E.**

The Atrahasis Story

"The Atrahasis Story" *deals primarily with creation and the earliest human history. It was originally composed in Sumerian, but was later copied and translated by the Babylonians and Assyrians in many editions.*

"The Atrahasis Story" *contains a flood episode, which is repeated in* "The Gilgamesh Story." *The most significant difference between the two episodes is the reason for the flood. There is no clear reason given in* "The Gilgamesh Story," *but in* "The Atrahasis Story," *the noise of an overpopulated earth is disturbing The Gods.*

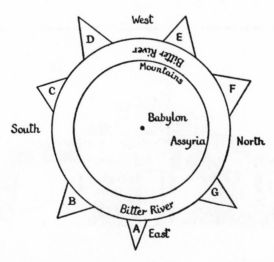

Fig. 7. **Clay tablet of about 2000 B.C.E. with a map of the world with Babylon at the center.**

They use a variety of means, like plague and famine, to cut down on the noise. Finally, they create a cataclysmic flood from which only Atrahasis and those in his ark survive.

"The Atrahasis Story" begins in a world populated only by The Gods. Eventually the younger and less important gods revolt, refusing to do all the work which is necessary to keep their world running properly. Ea-Enki negotiates a settlement with the younger gods in which humans will be created to take care of the world, especially by dredging its canals. The Divine Assembly of the Anunnaki—the old or inactive gods—ratify the proposal, but assign Nintu-Mami the actual task of carrying out the project.

Parallels between "The Atrahasis Story" and The Hebrew Bible include The Creation Story (Gen 2:4b—3:20), The Story of Noah and The Ark (Gen 6—8) and allusions to the work of midwives in various biblical texts.

[I]

Summon Nintu, the divine midwife!   192
    Let her deliver a newborn to labor for The Gods.
The Divine Assembly summoned the divine midwife,
    ... Mami the wise woman.
"Midwife the lullu!
    Deliver Aborigines to labor for The Gods!   195
Let them bear the yoke,
    Let them work for Enlil,
    Let them labor for The Gods."

"The Atrahasis Story" describes the labor of Nintu-Mami in great detail. The Divine Assembly's command to create workers who will take over the chores of the young gods is followed by several different accounts of how the task was actually carried out.

In one account the tellers compare Enki with a menstruating woman. He bathes three times during the menstrual cycle: first when the new moon appears, then seven days later, and finally fourteen days later when the full moon appears.

Nintu-Mami uses the body and the blood from We-ila to thin the clay. She manufactures the Aborigines just as a potter would shape a vessel, a bowl or a jar (Jer 18:2-6). When the vessel is finished, the midwife does not "name" her newborn "Alive," but summons them from the womb with the command: "Live!" (AH 1:216 + 229).

Nintu spoke,
   She said to The Divine Assembly:
"I have no authority,   200
   I cannot do Enki's work.
Only Enki has the jurisdiction,
   Only he has the clay I need!"
Enki spoke,
   He said to The Divine Assembly:
"At the new moon, on the seventh day, at the full moon
   I will bathe.
Let The Divine Assembly sacrifice a god.
   Let them be baptized.
Let Nintu thin the clay,   210
   ... with flesh and blood.
Let Nintu mix a human clay,
   ... with flesh and blood divine.
Let the drum mark off the days,
   ... count down the time.
Let this god's flesh make them live,
   Let the midwife command: Live!
   Let them have eternal life."
The Divine Assembly agreed,
   The Anunnaki consented.   220
At the new moon, on the seventh day, at the full moon Enki
     bathed.
The Divine Assembly sacrificed We-ila the Wise.
   ...
Nintu thinned the clay,
   ... with his flesh and blood.
The drum marked off the days,
   ... counted down the time.
This god's flesh made them live,
   The midwife commanded: Live!
   They had eternal life.   230

    *In another version, the midwife thins the clay with the saliva of
the Anunnaki and the Igigi.*

Nintu worked the clay,
   ... with saliva from the gods.
   ... from the Anunnaki,
   ... from the Igigi.

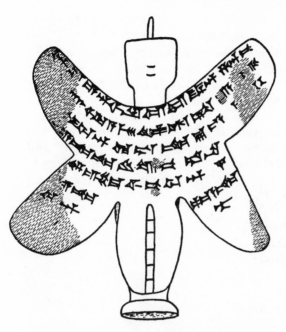

Fig. 8. **Late clay amulet with an inscription to the demon Pazazu across his body.**

Fig. 9. **Small amulet of the demon Pazazu, the bringer of disease.**

Mami spoke,
   She said to The Divine Assembly:
"You gave me a task;
   I have completed it.
You sacrificed a god,
   . . . We-ila the Wise.
I have assigned the lullu,
   To do the work of the Igigi.
You demanded Aborigines,
   . . .
I have loosened your yoke,
   I have set you free."
The Divine Assembly listened to Mami,
   The gods kissed her feet.
"Yesterday, we called you 'Mami,'
   Today, you are Mother of the living"
   (Gen 3:20).

240

In yet another version, Ea-Enki works the mixture, while Nintu-Mami sings. Once the mixture is thoroughly kneaded, Nintu-Mami cuts off fourteen pieces, shaping seven as males, seven as females (Gen 2:7). She beats a drum while the figures gestate. These actions can be easily enough translated into the movements of intercourse, but none is overtly described as sexual.

Tellers regularly portray their midwife characters with some kind of birthing stool. For example, when the pregnancy comes to term in "The Atrahasis Story," Nintu-Mami put on her cap and apron, "patterns the flour" (AH 1:287), and lays down the brick, before "opening the womb" (AH 1:282) and delivering the figures with the command "Live" (AH 1:216, 229).

They entered the labor room,
　. . . Ea the Prince, Mami the Wise.   *250*
She summoned the midwives,
　He worked the clay.
She sang the sacred song,
　He prayed the special prayer.
She finished singing,
　She pulled off fourteen pieces of clay.
She divided them into rows of seven,
　She set up the birth stool between the rows.
She summoned the midwives,
　She mounted the birth stool (Exod 1:16).   *260*
. . . .
She counted ten months,   *280*
　They determined her date.
The tenth month came,
　She went into labor.
Her face was beaming,
　. . . full of joy.
She put on her cap,
　She began to midwife.
She donned her apron,
　She began to pray.
She scattered the flour,
　She set up the birth stool.
"I have created,
　My hands gave life.
Let the midwife rejoice in the labor room,   *290*
　Where an expectant woman gives birth,

Where a woman births her child" (Gen 35:17; 1 Sam 4:20).
Erect the birth stool for nine days,
  Honor Nintu the Midwife . . . ,
Celebrate Mami continually,
  Praise The Midwife,
  Praise Kesh.
Let husband and wife lie together,   *300*
  . . . in their wedding bed.
Let husband and wife do what Ishtar commands,
  . . . in the father-in-law's house.
Celebrate for nine days,
  Honor Ishtar as "Ishara."

Rather than providing a comfort for the gods, however, the creation of human beings quickly led to an overpopulated earth and a cacophony that disturbed their sleep. Enlil decides that the way to cut down on the human population is through a plague.

In less than twelve hundred years. . . ,
The land was overpopulated,
  The people multiplied.
The land bellowed like a bull,
  The uproar disturbed The Gods.
When Enlil heard the noise,
  He complained to The Divine Assembly.
"I cannot stand this human uproar,
  I cannot sleep!
. . . .
  Send a plague upon the earth!"   *360*

King Atrahasis prays to Enki, his patron, for help and Enki teaches him how to end the plague.

"Command your messengers to proclaim,
  . . . to shout throughout the land—
"Do not worship The Gods,
  Do not pray to The Goddesses.
"Go to the gate of Namtar's temple,   *380*
  Place your finest loaf of bread on his threshold.
"Your gift of grain will please him,
  Your gift will shame him into withdrawing his hand."

Atrahasis persuaded The Elders to follow Enki's advice. They renovated the temple of Namtar—The God of Fate, placed their offering at the gate and Namtar stopped the plague.

Over the next six years, Enlil and The Divine Assembly try other means of controlling the human population. There is a drought and a famine. Then the soil becomes so salty that crops fail. An epidemic of skin disease—like psoriasis or shingles—and then malnutrition cripple the human population.

Each time, King Atrahasis appeals to Enki, who advises the people not to worship The Gods and The Goddesses and to make an offering only to the god responsible for their suffering. Each time, the strategy works and the god is shamed into sending the necessary relief which allows humanity to survive.

(II.i)

"I cannot stand this human uproar,
    I cannot sleep!
"Reduce their food supply,
    Let plants become scarce.   *10*
"Adad! Withhold the rain!
    Do not allow springs to rise from the deep.

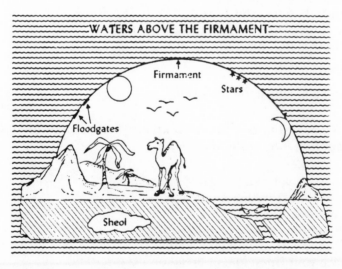

Fig. 10. An artist's portrayal of the universe as understood by the ancient semitic world.

"Winds! Blow the earth dry!
  Clouds! Gather, but do not rain
  (Isa 5:6).
"Let harvests be reduced,
  Let Nisaba, The Goddess of Grain, retard growth.
"Let the joy of the harvest, be gone!"

. . . .   *20*

(IV)

In the third year. . . ,   *11*
  Every human face was drawn with hunger.
Every human face was crusted like malt
  Every human lived on the brink of death.

. . . .

(S.vi)

In the fifth year. . . ,
A daughter stares while her mother goes into the house,
  . . . while her mother locks her out of the house.
A daughter stares while her mother is sold as a slave,
  A mother stares while her daughter is sold as a slave.   *10*
In the sixth year. . . ,
A daughter is cooked for dinner,
  A son is eaten for food.

But every effort of The Divine Assembly to reduce the human population is obstructed by Enki's advice to King Atrahasis.

(S.iv)

The people are not diminished,
  They are more numerous than ever.   *39*

In the face of Enki's opposition and aid to Atrahasis, The Divine Assembly determined that the only way to deal with the human population was a devastating flood. The Gods command Enki to take an oath that he will not reveal to Atrahasis how to save the humans from the flood. However, Atrahasis falls asleep in the temple of Enki. As the king begins to dream, Enki sits behind a lattice screen woven from reeds and begins to whisper his advice (1 Sam 3:3-4). Careful not to violate his oath, Enki does not speak to Atrahasis directly, but only to a wall, and Atrahasis thinks he has only dreamed of how to escape the flood.

(III.i)

"Listen to me, Wall!
  You Reed Mat, pay attention to me.
"Pull down your house,
  Build a barge.
"Abandon all your possessions,
  Save only your life.
"The barge should be . . .
  . . . equal . . .
"Place a roof over it,
  Cover it like Apsu, The Heavens, covers The Earth.
"Do not let The Sun see inside,
  Enclose it completely.
"Make the joints strong,
  Caulk the timbers with pitch.
"I will gather flocks of birds for your food,
  . . . and schools of fish for you to eat."
Then, Enki filled the water clock,
  Set the time for the flood on the seventh night.
King Atrahasis addressed The Elders: 40
  "My god has had a dispute with your god.
"Enki and Enlil are at odds,
  So I must leave this place.
"Since I worship Enki,
  I am a partner in this conflict.
"I can no longer live here,
  I can no longer dwell in the House of Enlil."

*With this as his explanation, Atrahasis proceeds to construct a
barge and fill it with all sorts of animals. Once he has it loaded, he
stages a banquet and sends his family on board. As he sits, sad-
dened by the impending flood, it begins to rain.*

The weather began to change. . . ,
Adad roared within the clouds.
  Atrahasis heard Adad's voice,   50
He closed the door
  And sealed it with pitch.
  (Gen 6:14)
Adad's roar filled the clouds,
  The winds blew fiercely.

Atrahasis cut the mooring rope,
  He let the barge float free.

(III.iii)

The noise in the land ceased,
  Like the silence following the breaking of a pot.   *10*
. . . .
The flood rushed forward,
  The flood charged the people like an army.
One person could not see the other,
  In the water no one was recognizable.
The flood bellowed like a bull,
  The winds howled like a wild ass braying.
. . . .
There was no sun,
  Only the darkness of the flood.   *20*
. . . .
The noise of the flood terrified The Gods.
Enki was furious,
  Seeing his children destroyed.
Nintu, The Lady,
  Bit her lips in anger.
The Anunnaki sat without food to eat,   *30*
  The Mighty went without wine to drink.
Mami The Wise wept at what she saw,
  The Divine Midwife broke into tears.

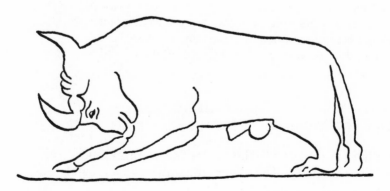

Fig. 11. **A bull on a bas relief from the ancient city of Enink.**

"How could I have agreed with The Divine Assembly?
  How could I have voted for a destruction so complete?
"Enlil's evil decree has gone too far,
  His words are worse than Tiruru   *40*
. . . .
"Where is Anu, Our Leader, now?
  Where are the humans to carry out his commands?
"Where is he who so thoughtlessly decreed a flood?
  . . . who condemned his own people to destruction?"

For seven days and seven nights the flood covered the earth.
Nintu and The Divine Assembly wept. Because the temples were
flooded and the humans were dead, there were no sacrifices for
them to eat or drink.
  Although the text is broken at this point, by comparison with
The Gilgamesh Story, it can be assumed that the flood subsided
and Atrahasis disembarked to prepare a sacrificial meal for The
Gods.

(III.v)

The Gods smelled the aroma,
  They swarmed like flies around his sacrifice.
  (Gen 8:21)
After The Gods had eaten their fill,
  Nintu indicted them all.
"Where is Anu, Our Leader, now?
  Why has this aroma not brought Enlil here?   *40*
"Where is he who so thoughtlessly decreed a flood?
  . . . who condemned his own people to destruction?"
"You decreed complete destruction,
  You darkened every shining face on the earth."
. . . .

(III.vi)

Enlil The Warrior saw the barge,
. . . .
Enlil was furious with The Igigi—The Younger Gods,
  "The Anunnaki, The Older Gods, all swore an oath!
"How could anyone survive that flood?
  How did this human escape destruction?"   *10*

(III.vii)

Anu immediately accused Enki of once again interfering with the will of the gods. Enki defends himself, but the final solution to the human population explosion is achieved when Enki and Nintu create women who are sterile, whose newborns die from crib death and who become celibate priestesses.

Let there be three new kinds of women . . .   *1*
Let some women be fertile,
   But let other women be sterile.
Let The Demon prey on the newborn,
   Let Pashittu steal infants from their mothers' laps.
Let there be women who are taboo,
   Let them be priestesses forbidden to have children.

The Story of Ra and The Serpent

Part of the daily responsibilites of every Egyptian priest was to chant creation stories to help Ra, The Sun God and every Pharaoh's patron, successfully navigate his barque through the night. During the journey, Apophis, The Divine Sea Serpent, tries to destroy Ra's barque.

The stories tell how every morning Ra recreates The Heavens and The Earth. Then Ra creates all the other gods who serve as his allies against Apophis, whom they paralyze with curses, thus allowing a new day to dawn and The Pharaoh to continue to rule Egypt in peace.

The text translated below comes from a 4th-century BCE papyrus, Papyrus Bremner-Rhind, but the story probably dates back to the Old Kingdom two thousand years earlier.

The principal parallel between "The Story of Ra and The Serpent" is found in "The Creation Story" in Gen 1:1—2:4a. Thus, only the section of "The Story of Ra and The Serpent" which deals with creation is translated here.

(XXVI)

Ra the Sun, The Almighty God, appeared and said: *21*
"I am Who Am!
   I am Khepri the Lifegiver!
   (Exod 3:14).
When I—Ra the Sun—appeared,
   Life appeared,

Every living creature appeared
  After I appeared.
There was no Heaven and no Earth (Gen 1:2),
  There was no Dry Land and no Reptiles in Egypt.
Then, I spoke and living creatures appeared (Gen 1:20–21).
  I put all of them to sleep in Nun, the primeval sea,
  Until I could find a place to stand.
When I began thinking about Egypt,
  ... began planning everything,
  ... began designing every creature by myself,
I had not exhaled Shu the Wind,
  I had not spat Tefnut the Rain,
  ... not a single living creature had appeared.
Then, I decided:
Let there be a multitude of living creatures (Gen 1:22),
  Let there be children and grandchildren."

Fig. 12. **The Sphinx from the tomb of King Chephren of the Fourth Dynasty in Giza. The Sphinx faces East and watches for the rising Sun to rule the world. About 2700 B.C.E.**

(XXVII)

"And so I copulated with my own fist,   *1*
  I masturbated with my own hand.
  I ejaculated into my own mouth.
I exhaled Shu the Wind,
  I spat Tefnut the Rain.
Old Man Nun, the primeval sea, reared them,
  Eye the Overseer looked after them
  . . . during the ages when I was away.
At first, I—Ra the Sun—was alone,
  Then, there were three more.
I—Ra the Sun—appeared here in Egypt,
  But Shu the Wind and Tefnut the Rain—played in Nun the
    primeval sea,
  And Eye the Overseer looked after them there.
After I had copulated with my own fist,
  I wept for joy.
Human beings appeared (Gen 2:6–7),
  From the tears which I shed.
Eye the Overseer was angry with me,
  For replacing it with another.
I had replaced Eye the Overseer,
  I had made Eye the Glorious.
I gave Eye the Overseer a place of honor,
  I made Eye the Overseer of all Egypt.
Tears of anger became tears of joy,
  What was lost had been recovered.

Fig. 13. **A scene of Egyptians tending both domestic cattle and wild antelope. From Beni Hasan (17th century B.C.E.).**

I took the tears of Eye the Overseer,
   and created all the Reptiles,
    ... and all their companions.
Shu the Wind and Tefnut the Rain gave birth to   *5*
   Geb the Earth and Nut the Sky.
Geb the Earth and Nut the Sky gave birth to
   the brothers: Osiris and Seth,
   and their wives; Isis and Nephthys,
   and Horus, son of Osiris and Isis.
One born right after another from the body of Geb the Earth,
   And they gave birth to all the people of Egypt."

The Memphis Creation Story

Originally a religious text composed sometime during the Old King-dom in Egypt, this version of "The Memphis Creation Story" comes from an 8th-century BCE copy. The text has elements of both a sa-cred drama, comparable to The Creation Story in Gen 1:1—2:4a, and a philosophical treatise describing the ordering of the world by Ptah The Creator and the establishment of Memphis as the center of his creation and as the capital of a united Egypt.

In this drama, The Ennead, the nine gods who are the chief deities of Egypt, are first called to recognize the unification of the country under the rule of The God Horus. Then Horus is combined in the person of The God Ptah, thereby making him both creator and supreme god among them. The powers and personalities of all the gods are then merged with that of Ptah to complete this process of creation and the reign of order.

Geb (the earth), Lord of The Gods, commanded that the Ennead assemble. He ended the dispute between Horus and Seth and divided the land between them with Horus receiving rule over Lower Egypt and Seth receiving rule over Upper Egypt.

Then Geb, realizing that Horus' portion should be greater than Seth's, increased his inheritance. He increased that of Horus, son of Osiris, who unified Upper and Lower Egypt.

As Osiris walked through The Gates of Death into the afterlife to rule there, his son Horus sat on the throne of Upper and Lower Egypt. And, at the urging of the goddesses Isis and Nephthys, Horus and Seth became as brothers and their quarrels ceased.

Ptah, the great god, gives life to all The Gods and to their ka-souls.

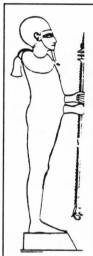

Fig. 14. **The gods Seth and Horus extend the symbol of life, the *ankh*, to an Egyptian man.**

Fig. 15. **The god Ptah, dressed as a mummy to signify that he is also lord of the underworld.**

They come into being through his heart and tongue, just as Horus came forth, Thoth came forth as Ptah. Ptah's heart and tongue thus rule and form the basis for all thought and all speech of all Gods, all men, and all that has life.

Ptah's Ennead serves as his teeth and lips. They are the semen and the hands of Atum, they came into being as he masturbated.

The Ennead is the teeth and lips which pronounced the names of all things (Gen 1:3) creating Shu (air) and Tefnut, who in turn gave birth to the Ennead.

All the senses—sight, hearing, smell—report to the heart. The heart is thus the source of all knowledge, the tongue speaks what the heart desires.

Thus all The Gods were made, his Ennead completed. Each word of God was spoken, by the decision of the heart, by the command of the tongue.

. . . .

Thus justice is done for the righteous and punishment to the disobedient. Thus life is granted to the calm in heart and death to the lawless one. Thus all crafts are created, all activities of hands and feet. All these things according to the command of the tongue and the decision of the heart.

Thus it is said of Ptah:

He made all and created The Gods. He is the one who gave birth to The Gods and from him comes forth all things. He is the mightiest of The Gods. Having done all these things, and being satisfied with them all, Ptah rested content with his work (Gen 1:31—2:2).

The Story of Gilgamesh

"The Story of Gilgamesh" celebrates the mighty deeds of Gilgamesh, Enkidu, Utnapishtim and others. Some characters in the story are human, some divine, some are both. For example, Gilgamesh, the king of Uruk, is one-third human and two-thirds divine. After his best friend—Enkidu—dies, the king sets out on a quest for immortality. The story tells of all the mighty deeds which Gilgamesh performs on his journey to Dilmun, where the once mortal Utnapishtim and his wife now live as immortals.

In 1872 archaeologists found a copy of "The Story of Gilgamesh" at Nineveh in Iraq. It was written in cuneiform on twelve baked clay tablets. On the eleventh tablet, Utnapishtim tells Gilgamesh how he and his wife became immortal by surviving a great flood in a giant cube-shaped barge. When The Divine Assembly discovered some mortals had survived the flood, they voted to change Utnapishtim and his wife from mortals into immortals in order not to violate their own decree that no mortals survive the flood!

In the Babylonian telling of the story, Atrahasis is the protagonist; in the Sumerian version, Ziusudra is the hero. Ancient Israel retells the Utnapishtim episode of "The Story of Gilgamesh" in "The Story of Noah and the Ark!" (Gen 6—8). The similarities and the differences in these stories emphasize the similarities and differences between Israel and her ancient Near Eastern neighbors.

Tell me, Utnapishtim, how did you and your wife become immortal and join The Divine Assembly?

Well, Gilgamesh, let me tell you the story of a divine conspiracy, a secret plot which The Gods devised to exterminate humanity. *10*

Fig. 16. **The demon Humbaba who guarded the sacred Cedar tree of the gods, and whom Gilgamesh and Enkidu slew. Enkidu was condemned to death for such deeds, which triggered Gilgamesh's search for immortality.**

The Gods decided to flood The Earth. But Ea, God of Fresh Water, whispered to the reed walls of my house the plans of Enlil, Leader of The Divine Assembly.   *20*

Listen to me, Wall!
  You Reed Mat, pay attention to me.
Pull down your house,
  Build a barge.
Abandon all your possessions,
  Save only your life!

Take specimens of every living thing on board. Make the ark as wide as it is long (Gen 6:11-21), with a roof like the dome of the   *30*
heavens.
  I told Ea that I would obey his orders, but then asked: "What shall I tell the people and the elders of the city?" He said: "Tell them: I have learned that Enlil has sentenced me to death, so I cannot stay   *40*
here in Shurippak, his city, but must move to the coast where Ea is lord."
  First, I built the hulls of the ark one-hundred seventy-five feet high, and the decks one-hundred seventy-five feet wide. I constructed a top deck and six lower decks, separated into compartments by   *60*
nine bulkheads. Then I caulked the ark with bitumen and asphalt thinned with oil (Gen 6:14-16). I fed my workers as if it were festival   *70*
time and the ark was completed in seven days. We had a difficult

time launching the ark, but we finally managed to get it into the water using log rollers.

Then I loaded all my gold and silver, my entire family, domes- *80* tic animals, wild beasts, and all kinds of craftspeople into the ark (Gen 7:2-4 + 7-9). Finally, at the precise moment set by Shamash, God of the Sun, I boarded the ark, battened down the hatch and *90* turned command of the ark and its manifest over to Puzur-Amurri, the navigator (Gen 7:13-16).

At dawn. . . ,
The Horizons turned black with clouds,
    Adad, God of Thunder, roared.
Shullat and Hanish—The Divine Messengers—
    Flew over hill and plain.   *100*
Nergal, God of the Underworld, unlocked The Cosmic Dam.
    Ninurta, Son of Enlil, opened The Dikes.
The Gods strafed The Earth with lightning,
    Adad turned The Day into Night.
Throughout the day. . . ,
The Winds attacked like soldiers,
    The Waters drowned the mountains and the people
    (Gen 7:11-12 + 17-23).   *110*

Fig. 17. **The second figure from the right is probably the god Anu holding the waters of life, which he passes in a vase to a naked Gilgamesh. The small animals and objects represent the constellations of stars.**

One person could not see the other,
   The Heavens could not see The Earth.
The Waters ran The Anunnaki into The Heavens,
   Frightened The Gods like stray dogs against city walls.
Ishtar, Goddess of Love and War, shrieked,
   Cried out like a woman in labor (Mic 4:9):
"How could I kill my own people,   *120*
   Conspire with The Gods against those
   to whom I gave birth?
Their bodies float on the sea,
   Swell like schools of dead fish."
The Anunnaki sat humbled,
   The Gods wept.

For six days and six nights the winds blew. On the seventh day, the raging storm subsided and the sea grew quiet. I felt the stillness *130* and then realized that everyone else had drowned in the flood. I opened the hatch, and sunlight fell on my face. I bowed my face to the deck and wept with tears running down my cheeks (Gen 7:24—8:3).

The ark ran aground on Mount Nisir (Gen 8:4). It remained *140* grounded for six days and, then, on the seventh day I released a dove. It flew back and forth, but came back without finding a place to rest. Then I released a swallow, but it also returned without find- *150* ing a place to rest. Finally, I released a raven. Because the flood waters had begun to subside, the raven fed, circled, cawed and flew away. Immediately, I released the rest of the creatures from the ark and they scattered to the four winds (Gen 8:5-17).

I prepared a sacrifice,
   I poured a libation on the mountaintop.
I set out my sacred vessels,
   I kindled a sacred fire of reed, cedar and myrtle.
The Gods smelled the aroma,   *160*
   They swarmed like flies around the sacrifice
   (Gen 8:20).

When Ishtar arrived, she removed her necklace of lapis-lazuli and took this oath:

"By my necklace, I swear,
   I shall never forget these days.

Fig. 18. **Gilgamesh, naked, fights with Enkidu, half-man, half-beast on the left. The goddess Ishtar stands on the far right. A cylinder seal from the time of Hammurabi (18th century B.C.E.).**

Let every god enjoy this meal,
    But let Enlil eat no sacrifice mortals prepare.
Enlil thoughtlessly created a flood,
    He drowned the mortals who feed The Gods!"
    (Gen 8:21–22 + 9:12–17).

But, when Enlil did arrive and saw the ark, he was furious: *170*

"Have some mortals escaped?
    Every last one was to be destroyed!"

Consequently, Ninurta convened The Divine Assembly and indicted Ea for obstructing Enlil's plan to flood the earth. Ea opened his defense by reiterating that he only wanted to control the human population with wild animals, famine, or plague, not destroy every last mortal with a flood. In closing, Ea testified:

"I did not tell Utnapishtim of Enlil's plan,
    I did not warn him of the impending doom.
Subpoena Utnapishtim,
    Let the mortal speak.
He dreamed a dream alone,
    He interpreted the divine conspiracy for himself."

Eventually, based on the decision of The Divine Assembly, Enlil boarded the ark and told me and my wife to kneel on either side of him. He laid his hands on our heads and decreed:

"Utnapishtim and his wife have been mortal,
    Henceforth they shall be immortal.
They shall live in a far away land,
    They shall dwell at The Mouth of the Rivers!"
    (Gen 9:1–17).
So, The Gods resettled us in this far away land,
    They brought us to The Mouth of the Rivers.

So, this concludes the story of how we became immortal. Now, Gilgamesh, you have to tell my wife and me the story how you are going to become immortal and join The Divine Assembly.

Fig. 19. **A statue of Gilgamesh holding a lion cub (Louvre).**

Fig. 20. **A nude statue of the goddess Ishtar from the early Babylonian period.**

The Story of Anubis and Bata

Twins, brothers or rivals regularly appear in the creation stories of both eastern Mediterranean cultures like Egypt or Israel and western Mediterranean cultures like Greece. Storytellers use the twins-motif to discuss how life and death began. Multiple births characterize the epoch primeval as a time when life was abundant. However, the sibling rivalry of this period sets deadly violence in motion.

By 1860, archaeologists had recovered an Egyptian telling of this kind of story which was popular in 1225 BCE. It was written on papyrus paper, not in hieroglyphic characters, but in a cursive style of Egyptian writing called "hieratic."

Parallels to "The Story of Anubis and Bata" *in ancient Israel appear in* "The Story of Cain and Abel (Gen 4:1–26)" *and* "The Story of Joseph and Potiphar (Gen 39:1–21)." *The rivalry between an older and a younger brother also parallels* "The Story of Cain and Abel" *and* "The Story of Jacob and Esau" *(Gen 26–27). The talking animal who saves the life of its master is found in* "The Story of Balaam" *(Num 22:28–30). And finally, the propositioning of a servant by the master's wife parallels* "The Story of Joseph and Potiphar."

Now there were two brothers: Anubis was the older, Bata the younger. But Anubis was a free man, who was married and owned his own home; Bata, however, was his brother's ward, living with him like a son. He lived in the house which Anubis owned, wore the clothes which Anubis made for him, tended Anubis' cattle, plowed Anubis' fields, brought in Anubis' harvest and did all Anubis' field-

41

Fig. 21. **Egyptians plowing with the use of oxen. From tomb 2 at Beni Hasan (19th century B.C.E.).**

work! The younger brother was a righteous man, blameless in his generation. He had the creator's power within him.

(i)

One day, after Bata finished his chores herding the cattle, he   5
headed home loaded down with vegetables, milk, firewood—everything he needed to prepare supper for Anubis and his wife. After supper, Bata went out to the barn to sleep with the cattle.

The next morning, Bata got up and cooked breakfast for Anubis and his wife, and packed his brother's lunch. Then Bata drove the cattle out into the pasture to graze. As Bata walked alongside the cattle, they would say to him: "The grass in this pasture is excellent," and Bata would listen to the cattle and drive them to whichever pasture they wanted to graze. . . .

(ii)

. . . So Anubis' cattle became prime livestock, calving twice as   1
often as ordinary livestock (Gen 30:40–2).

Now when it was plowing time, Anubis told Bata: "Tomorrow is the first day of plowing. Be sure the oxen are ready to be yoked and the seed is ready to be planted, first thing in the morning."

The younger brother did everything his older brother told him to do.   5

At the break of dawn, Anubis and Bata hurried to the fields with their seed in order to start plowing. They were delighted with how well the work was going.

After a while, they ran short of seed. So Anubis sent his younger brother to the village to get some more. When Bata got to the house, Anubis' wife was sitting there combing out her hair. Bata said to her: "Get up and give me some seed. . . ,

(iii)

... my older brother is waiting for me. Hurry!" Then she said to *1*
him: "Go and open the bin and take what you want! I am not
finished combing my hair."

Then Bata went to the barn, took a big jar and filled it with
barley and emmer seed and hoisted the jar on his shoulders.

When Anubis' wife saw Bata, she said: "How much seed are
you carrying?" and Bata answered: "Three measures of emmer, two *5*
measures of barley: five in all." Then she said: "My, you are certainly strong. Everyday I notice your bulging muscles." She wanted
to have intercourse with him (Gen 39:7).

Suddenly Anubis' wife jumped up and threw her arms around
Bata. "Come on now, sleep with me just this once, and I will sew
some new clothes for you," she pleaded (Gen 39:12).

Bata was as furious as a leopard at the very thought of sleeping
with his brother's wife. His anger terrified her. "You have got to be
crazy!" he shouted at her. "You and your husband are like a mother
and father to me. Because he was older than I, he reared me. How
. . .

(iv)

... can you possibly suggest I commit a crime like this against *1*
him? Listen, if you promise never to proposition me again like this, I
won't tell anyone what you said."

Then Bata shouldered the seed and left for the field. He re-
joined his brother, and they worked hard all day together.

When the sun set, Anubis left for home, while Bata the Younger
tended his cattle and picked up all the equipment. Then he drove
his cattle home so that they could sleep in their own barn in the *5*
village.

Fig. 22. **Egyptians harvesting flax and doing other agricultural chores.
From tomb 2 at Beni Hasan (19th century B.C.E.).**

Meanwhile, Anubis' wife was afraid of getting into trouble for what she had done. So she drank a mixture of fat and grease to make herself sick.... She did not trim, nor light the lamps when it got dark, and she did not bring Anubis any water to wash his hands when he got home ... she just lay there vomiting....

... she told Anubis....

(v)

"When your brother came back for some seed, I was here alone. *1* He propositioned me: 'Come on now, let your hair down and sleep with me just this once!' But I would not pay any attention to him. 'Aren't I like a mother to you?' I pleaded. 'Isn't your older brother like a father to you?' But he panicked and beat me so that I would not tell you. Now, if you let him live, I'll kill myself!" (Gen 39: 17–19) ....

Anubis was furious as a leopard. He fetched his spear, sharp- *5* ened its point and stood behind the barn door to wait for Bata to return with the cattle later that evening.

... however, when the first cow went into the barn, she warned Bata: "Your older brother is waiting to kill you with his spear. Run!" (Num 22:28–30). ... As soon as Bata looked under the door of the barn and saw his older brother's feet, ... he dropped his load and ran. His older brother chased him with his spear.

Bata began to pray: "My lord, Ra-Harakhti...,

(vi)

... only you are good enough to judge between the just and the *5* unjust." The moment Ra heard his prayer, he created a lake full of crocodiles which protected Bata from his older brother....

Fig. 23. **Egyptians leading cattle back to the barns. From tomb 3 at Beni Hasan (19th century B.C.E.).**

When it was dawn and The Sun Disk rose over The Horizon, Bata argued his case with his older brother [in the presence of The Sun God Ra] (Jer 7:2–4). "Why are you hunting me? Why do you want to kill me without giving me a chance to speak in my defense? I am still your younger brother.

(vii)

You and your wife are like father and mother to me. . . ." Then 5
Bata told him everything that had happened. He finished his story with an oath and an ordeal.

"So help me Ra-Harakhti, only a dirty, lying whore could get you to take up your spear and try to kill me for no reason at all!" Then, he took his knife and cut off his own penis and threw it into the lake where a catfish swallowed it. . . .

(viii)

So, Bata the Younger went into exile in Lebanon, the Valley of the Cedar, and Anubis the Elder set off for home in mourning. He 7
struck his forehead with his hand and smeared his face with dirt. When he got home, he killed his wife and fed her body to the dogs (2 Kgs 9:36). Then he sat in mourning for his younger brother. . . .

The Book of Exodus

The Treaty of Ramses II
and Hattusilis III
Egyptian Edition

For more than one hundred years, Egypt and Hatti struggled for control of the eastern Mediterranean. The conflict drained the resources of both superpowers. About 1280 BCE, following the famous, but inconclusive, battle at Kadesh—located in today's Syria—"The Treaty of Ramses II and Hattusilis III" was signed. This treaty was a remarkable political and military accomplishment. It was motivated both by Egypt's and Hatti's need for economic recovery, as well as the increasing military threat of The Sea Peoples migrating across the islands of today's Greece and into the eastern Mediterranean. The treaty kept the peace for virtually the next fifty years.

In the early 1900s archaeologists recovered both Egyptian and Hittite editions of the treaty. In the Egyptian edition, Ramses II flamboyantly elaborates on the role which he played in negotiating the treaty in order to use it as a public-relations tool. He had one copy carved in hieroglyphics on walls of The Temple of Amon in Karnak and another on the walls of his own funeral chapel, The Ramesseum, in The Valley of the Kings—both located near today's Luxor in central Egypt. The Hittite edition is a more sober legal document written on clay tablets in cuneiform, using Akkadian, which was the diplomatic language of the ancient Near East. Archaeologists recovered the tablets from the archives of Hattusas, the Hittite capital—located in today's Turkey.

The Hittites developed the treaty form, which other cultures used as need arose. Standard Hittite treaties contained at least six components. They opened by giving the credentials of the signato-

ries to the treaty and issuing a new and official history of the countries affected by it. Then they laid out the terms in careful legal language. These were followed by a list of witnesses to the treaty, a litany of curses for treaty violations and blessings for treaty compliance, and finally provisions to record and promulgate the treaty.

The Israelite covenant genre parallels the Hittite treaty in many ways. Simple covenants appear in negotiations between Jacob and Laban in Genesis 31:44–54; major covenants appear in "The Covenant Code" from The Book of Exodus, "The Holiness Code" from The Book of Leviticus and "The Deuteronomic Code" from The Book of Deuteronomy.

Credentials

Inscribed on this silver tablet is the treaty creating peace and eternal alliance between Hattusilis, Great King of Hatti—son of Mursilis, Great King of Hatti, Grandson of Suppiluliumas, Great King of Hatti—and Ramses, The Pharaoh of Egypt—Son of Seti, The Pharaoh of Egypt, Son of Ramses, The Pharaoh of Egypt.

History

In the beginning, The Gods decreed that there be peace between The Pharaoh of Egypt and The Great King of Hatti. But, Muwatallis, my brother and The Great King of Hatti, declared war on Ramses. However, from this day forward, Hattusilis will observe the decree of Ra and Seth, which prohibits war between Egypt and Hatti forever.

Terms

Current Relations

Hattusilis agrees to this treaty with Ramses, creating peace and an eternal alliance between us. We are brothers and are at peace with each other forever.

I, Hattusilis, came to the throne of Hatti, when Muwatallis died. Therefore, I agree to this treaty with Ramses, creating peace and an alliance between us. The state of peace and alliance between our lands is now better than in former times.

I, Ramses, agree to peace and an alliance. The successors of The Great King of Hatti will be allies with the successors of Ramses. The relationship between Egypt and Hatti shall be like our relationship—one of peace and an eternal alliance. There will never again be war between us.

Mutual Non-Aggression

In the future, The Great King of Hatti shall neither invade, nor raid Egypt, and Ramses shall neither invade, nor raid Hatti.

Reaffirmation of Former Treaties

I, Hattusilis, reaffirm the treaties of Suppiluliumas and of Muwatallis, Great Kings of Hatti. I, Ramses, affirm the treaty I make with Hattusilis today, and will observe it and act accordingly from now on.

Defensive Alliance

If a foreign army invades the lands of Ramses, and he sends a message to The Great King of Hatti, saying: "Come and help me against this enemy," The Great King of Hatti shall come and fight against the enemy of Egypt, his ally. If The Great King of Hatti does not wish to come personally, he may send infantry and chariots to fight against the enemy of Egypt, his ally.

Likewise, if Ramses is trying to put down an armed revolt, The Great King of Hatti shall help him until all the rebels have been executed.

If a foreign army attacks The Great King of Hatti, Ramses shall come and fight against the enemy of Hatti, his ally. If Ramses does not wish to come personally, he may send infantry and chariots, as well as word to this effect, to Hatti. If the officials of The Great King of Hatti break their oaths of loyalty to him, Ramses. . . .

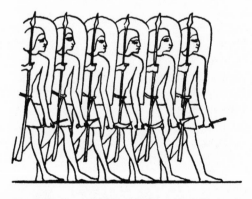

Fig. 24. **The infantry of Pharaoh Rameses II on the march.**

Orderly Succession

The Egyptian edition of the treaty is fragmented here, the following translation combines both The Egyptian edition and The Hittite edition.

When Hattusilis dies, The Son of Hattusilis shall be crowned Great King of Hatti in his father's place. If the officials of Hatti revolt against his son, Ramses shall send infantry and chariots to avenge Hattusilis (2 Kgs 9:16–26). Once order has been restored in Hatti, they shall return to Egypt. . . .

If there was a reciprocal clause for Egyptian succession, it has been lost at this point in damage to both texts.

Extradition

The Great King of Hatti shall not grant asylum to any citizen of Egypt who is a fugitive from justice. The Great King of Hatti shall have the fugitive extradited to Ramses. Likewise, any runaway slave, who escapes to Hatti in search of a new master, shall be extradited to Ramses.

The Pharaoh of Egypt shall not grant asylum to any citizen of Hatti who is a fugitive from justice. The Pharaoh of Egypt shall have the fugitive extradited to The Great King of Hatti. Likewise, any runaway slave who escapes to Egypt in search of a new master, shall be extradited to The Great King of Hatti.

List of Witnesses

All The Gods of Hatti and Egypt are witnesses to this treaty between The Great King of Hatti and Ramses inscribed on this silver tablet.

Ra, God of the Sky
Ra, God of Arinna
Seth, God of the Storm
Seth, God of Hatti
Seth, God of Arinna
Seth, God of Zippalanda
Seth, God of Pettiyarik
Seth, God of Hissashapa
Seth, God of Sarissa
Seth, God of Aleppo
Seth, God of Lihzina
The God of Zitharias
The God of Karzis
The God of Hapantaliyas

The Goddess of Karahna
The Queen of the Sky
The Gods of Oaths
The Goddess of the Earth
Ishara, The Lady of Oaths
Ishara, The Lady of Mountains and Rivers of Hatti
The Gods of Kizuwadna
Amon Ra
Seth
The Gods of the Mountains and Rivers of Egypt
The Sky
The Earth
The Sea
The Winds
The Clouds
(Gen 31:51–53)

Litany of Curses and Blessings

Cursed by The Gods of Hatti and Egypt be the homes, and lands and slaves of those who do not observe the treaty between Hatti and Egypt inscribed on this silver tablet.

Blessed by The Gods of Hatti and Egypt with prosperity and long life be the homes and lands and slaves of those Egyptians and Hittites who observe and carry out faithfully the treaty between Hatti and Egypt inscribed on this silver tablet (Gen 31:45–50). . . .

Fig. 25. **Rameses II.**

Fig. 26. **The Hittite God Teshub.**

Fig. 27. A bronze head from the Old Akkadian period, presumably the head of Sargon of Akkad. One of the finest pieces of third millennium Mesopotamian art.

The Story of Sargon's Birth

Sometime after 3000 BCE, the ancient city of Akkad was founded near the present city of Baghdad, Iraq. Agriculture, trade and war soon made Akkad a great city, and Sargon of Agade (2371–2316 BCE) one of its greatest rulers.

By 1900 archaeologists had recovered three copies which were made of "The Story of Sargon's Birth," which celebrated the humble beginnings of this great leader. A parallel to "The Story of Sargon's Birth" appears in The Book of Exodus (Exod 1:22—2:10), which celebrates the humble-beginnings motif of Moses as one of ancient Israel's greatest leaders.

Call me Sargon. The child of a priestess and an unknown pilgrim from the mountains, I now rule a Mesopotamian Empire from my capital in Agade.

Because my mother was a priestess who would be expected to offer her children as sacrifices, she did not want anyone in the city of Asupiranu to know that she had conceived and given me birth. Therefore, she hid me along the bank of the Euphrates River in a basket woven from rushes and waterproofed with tar.

The river carried my basket down to an irrigation canal where Akki, the royal gardener, lifted me out of the water and reared me as his own. Akki trained me to become his assistant in the royal gardens.

With the help of Ishtar, goddess of love and war, I rose to the position of king of the black-headed people in just over four years. I then campaigned in every land from the Armenian mountains west to the Mediterranean sea, from the land of Dilmun on the Persian

Gulf to the port of Dor on the Mediterranean coast. Three times I marched from the Persian Gulf to the Mediterranean blazing trails through the mountains with bronze-headed axes; scaling peaks, crossing valleys, conquering ports like Dor and cities like Kazallu.

To my successors I leave this as a legacy.

The Books of
Leviticus, Numbers,
Deuteronomy

The Story of Balaam

Hendricus Jacobus Franken excavated Deir 'Alla in the Jordan Valley in 1967. First, a bit of plaster with writing in red and black ink on it, and then two large fragmentary inscriptions were recovered. The plaster may have been applied to a stele or the walls of a sanctuary dedicated to the gods named in the prophecy and intended to protect the community from the kind of natural disasters described in the story. "The Story of Balaam" is written in a dialect of the Aramaic language common in the southern part of Canaan. The artifacts found with the plaster and the style of writing date it to ca 700 BCE.

The fragments of plaster have been reassembled by scholars in more than one sequence. In the first combination, translated below, Balaam, the son of Beor, has a dream that his city is about to be destroyed. The destruction was planned by The Gods, who would cause the order of nature in the city to be reversed. For example, tame animals became wild and wild animals became tame. Poor women were using myrrh as though they were rich. The next morning Balaam was sad. When asked about it, he told about his dream. It would seem the plan was averted and the city saved, which teaches the audience that it is possible to make peace with The Gods and prevent a disaster altogether or at least minimize its effects. Nonetheless, Balaam himself is condemned to death for thwarting the plans of the gods.

There are parallels to the world-turned-upside-down motif in "The Story of Balaam" in laments from The Book of Lamentations. Likewise, the motif in which a divine patron warns a human protégé of an impending disaster also appears in "The Atrahasis Story," "The Story of Gilgamesh" and The Story of Noah and The Ark (Gen 6–8). Finally, the Balaam, son of Beor, character also appears as a prophet in Numbers 22:5—24:25.

Fig. 28. **Antelopes grazing on shrubs. From a Canaanite vase found near Ziklag. Late Bronze Age.**

This is "The Story of Balaam," son of Beor and a seer for The Gods (1 Sam 9:11). The Gods appear to him at night. He sees a vision and receives an oracle from El. They tell Balaam, son of Beor, that a fire which cannot be extinguished—a drought which will never end—is coming.

Balaam gets up the next morning, but he is unable to eat and he weeps bitterly. The people in his city approach him and ask: *5*
"Balaam, son of Beor, why do you fast?
  Why do you cry?"
Then Balaam tells them about his vision.
"Be seated!
Let me tell you what The *Shadday* have done,
  Let me show you what The Gods have decided.
  (Exod 6:3)
The *Shadday* convened The Divine Assembly,
  They said to The Gods. . . .
Lock up the heavens,
  Bolt the doors of the clouds.
Bring darkness,
  Instead of light
  (Joel 2:10; Lam 3:2).
Seal the doors,
  Bolt them shut forever!

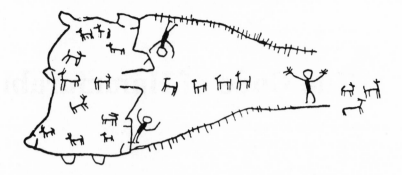

Fig. 29. **A sheepfold made from brambles and perhaps mud for holding the flocks at night while on the move. This one is from a stone graffito from Transjordan.**

The swift competes with the eagle for food,
    The voice of the vulture cries out . . .
For the stork . . . the young of the cormorant bird,
    . . . claws the marsh bird and the sparrow.   *10*
The shepherd's staff herds rabbits instead of sheep,
. . . .
The hyena is tame,
    The fox pup runs wild.
The poor woman perfumes herself with myrrh,
    The priestess . . .
    (Exod 30:23–33).
The prince wears tattered clothes,
    (Lam 2:10).
. . . .
Those once respected, now show respect,
    Those who once showed respect are now respected.
. . . the deaf hear long distance,
    . . . the fool sees visions."
. . . .

   The remaining fragments of The Story of Balaam continue to describe how everything in the city is backwards.

The Code of Hammurabi

"The Code of Hammurabi" *is a treatise on legal theory, political science and social organization. Hammurabi, emperor of Babylon from 1792–1750 BCE, published this classic to endorse the legal thinking and moral values of his government. In 1901, French excavators recovered a copy of* "The Code of Hammurabi" *at Susa on the border between Iraq and Iran. It was inscribed in cuneiform on an eight-foot pillar of black diorite.*

A catalog of Hammurabi's military victories and political endorsements introduces two hundred eighty-two case laws. Each case law has two parts. First, a dependent clause introduced by the conjunction "if" describes a situation: "If one citizen charges another with murder, without the evidence to prove it...." Second, a main clause introduced by the adverb "then" imposes a sentence: "... then the plaintiff is to be sentenced to death" (CH 1). Distinct socioeconomic groups, such as slaves, citizens and members of the political or religious establishment, appear in the laws. An essay on the role of justice in any successful government concludes the treatise.

In ancient Israel, "The Covenant Code" (Exod 21—23), "The Holiness Code" (Lev 17—26) and "The Deuteronomic Code" (Deut 12—26) reflect similarities to and differences from "The Code of Hammurabi." These parallels either result from direct contact between the cultures of Babylon and Israel, or simply demonstrate that two cultures with some shared values develop similar procedures for resolving the same judicial questions.

Article 1

If one citizen charges another with murder, without the evidence to prove it, then the plaintiff is sentenced to death (Exod 23:1–3; Deut 19:16–19).

62

Fig. 30. **A cylinder seal from the city of Alalakh in northern Syria. The owner says that he was a subject of the king of Karana, but the arrow-shaped spade between the figures suggests the symbol of Marduk and probably indicates that both cities were subject to Hammurabi of Babylon.**

Article 8
If a citizen steals an ox or a sheep from an official of the government or the temple, then the fine is thirty times the value of the stolen livestock; likewise, if one citizen steals an ox or a sheep from another, then the fine is ten times the value of the stolen livestock; however, if a thief fails to pay the fine imposed for stealing livestock, then the sentence is death (Exod 20:15; Deut 5:19; 22:1–4; Lev 19:11 + 13).

Article 14
If a citizen kidnaps and sells a member of another citizen's household into slavery, then the sentence is death (Exod 21:16; Deut 24:7).

Article 21
If one citizen tunnels through the wall of another's house and robs it, then the sentence is death. The execution shall take place outside the tunnel, and the convict's body used to fill in the tunnel (Exod 22:2–3).

Article 117
If a citizen sells his wife, his son, his daughter or himself into slavery to pay a debt, then the creditor cannot contract for more

than three years service and must free them at the beginning of the
fourth year (Exod 21:2-11; Deut 15:12-18).

Article 120
If a citizen swears an oath at the temple that his grain was
destroyed or stolen by the granary owner who was storing it, then
the owner is fined two times the value of the missing grain (Exod
22:7-8).

Article 129
If the wife of one citizen is caught having sexual intercourse
with another, then both are sentenced to the ordeal of being tied and
thrown into the river; however, if the woman's husband grants her a
pardon, then the monarch can pardon her partner (Deut 22:22).

Article 130
If a citizen is caught raping a woman, who is marriageable,
engaged and still living with her parents, then the man shall be
sentenced to death, but the woman shall be exonerated (Deut
22:23-7).

Article 132
If the wife of a citizen is charged with, but not actually caught
having sexual intercourse with another, then she is sentenced to the
ordeal of throwing herself into the river in order to exonerate her
husband (Num 5:11-31); if she survives the ordeal, then she shall
pay a fine (Ur-Nammu 10-11).

Article 144
If a citizen, who is married to a Naditu priestess, is given a slave
by his wife and she [the slave] bears him children, then he may not
marry a lay priestess (Gen 16:1-15; 21:9-21).

Article 145
If a citizen is married to a Naditu priestess who does not contract with a slave to bear his children, then he may marry a lay
priestess, but her legal standing is inferior to the Naditu (Gen 16:1-
15; 21:9-21).

Article 146
If the slave with whom a Naditu priest has a contract to bear
her husband's children considers herself to have the same legal

Fig. 31. The basalt
stele of Hammurabi
listing his law code.

Fig. 32. A drawing of the top of Hammurabi's
stele showing the king before the sun god
Shamash.

standing as the Naditu once she has borne children, then the
Naditu may brand her and reduce her to the status of a household
slave, but she may not sell her (Gen 16:1–15; Gen 21:9–21).

Article 147

If the slave with whom a Naditu priest has a contract to bear
her husband's children considers herself to have the same legal
standing as the Naditu even though she has not had children, then
the Naditu may sell her (Gen 16:1–15; Gen 21:9–21).

Article 154

If a citizen has sexual intercourse with his daughter, then the
sentence is exile from the city (Lev 18:6–18; 20:10–21; Deut 27:20 +
22–23).

Article 170

If a citizen who has children by his wife and by his slave adopts the slave's children, then his estate shall be divided evenly between the children of both, after his wife's first-born son receives the preferential share (Gen 21:9–21).

Article 195

If a citizen strikes his father, then the sentence is the amputation of a hand (Exod 21:15).

Article 196

If a citizen blinds an eye of a member of the establishment, then the sentence is the blinding of an eye.

Article 197

If one citizen breaks a bone of another, then the sentence is the breaking of a bone.

Article 198

If a citizen blinds the eye or breaks the bone of someone who is not a citizen, the fine is eighteen ounces of silver.

Fig. 33. **A cylinder seal showing the sun god Shamash rising from behind the mountains. The goddess Ishtar stands over him, and the god Baal or Adad pours out the rains to his right. On the left, Shamash is shown again as a hunter. From the Sumerian period.**

Article 199

If one citizen blinds the eye or breaks the bone of another citizen's slave, the fine is one-half the slave's value (Lev 24:19–20; Exod 21:23–25; Deut 19:21).

Article 209

If one citizen beats the daughter of another and causes her to miscarry, then the fine is six ounces of silver (Sumerian Laws 1; Exod 21:22–3).

Article 251

If a member of the aristocracy is gored by the ox of an ordinary citizen, who neither tethered the animal, nor blunted its horns, even after the city council put the owner on notice that the animal was dangerous, then the owner's fine is eighteen ounces of silver (Exod 21:28–36).

The Sumerian Code

Ur-Nammu, who ruled in Ur III from 2113–2096 BCE, authorized the publication of "The Ur-Nammu Code," *which is the oldest ancient Near Eastern law code recovered by archaeologists. It establishes an enduring legal tradition to which* "The Sumerian Code" *from 1800 BCE belongs. The tradition applies uniform principles of justice to a wide range of social institutions—from the standardization of weights and measures, on the one hand, to the protection of widows and orphans, on the other. For example, sentences in the case laws of* "The Ur-Nammu Code" *are generally determined by the principle of restitution paid to the victim, rather than by the principle of revenge taken on the convict.*

Fig. 34. **A plaque of King Ur-Ninu of Lagash showing his cupbearer and four sons. Sumerian period.**

"The Ur-Nammu Code" *and the cuneiform language in which it was written were the most important subjects studied by candidates for government jobs in Sumer. In practice texts like* "The Sumerian Code," *candidates wrote out, again and again, the technical terms and phrases from* "The Ur-Nammu Code" *which would appear in the examinations at the end of their training.*

Parallels to "The Sumerian Code" *in ancient Israel appear in* "The Deuteronomic Code" *(Deut 12—26).*

Article 4

If a son disowns his father and mother with the oath: "You are not my father; you are not my mother," then he forfeits his right to inherit their property; likewise, he can then be sold as an ordinary slave [—not just indentured for three years to pay a debt—] at full market value (Deut 21:18-21).

Article 8

If the daughter of a citizen, with her parents' knowledge, walks about the city and is raped, then the rapist, if he swears an oath at the temple gate that he did not know she was a free-born woman, shall not be charged (Gen 34; Exod 22:16; Deut 22:23-4).

The Hittite Code

"The Hittite Code" *represents legal thinking in the Empire of Hatti between 1450–1200 BCE. After 1893 archaeologists excavated some 10,000 baked clay tablets from Hattusas, the 419-acre site of the Hittite capital, now in central Turkey. They included samples of* "The Hittite Code." *These two hundred case laws were written on two baked clay tablets in Neshili Hittite using cuneiform script. By 1915, Bedrich Hrozny, a Czech scholar, was able to translate the language.*

"The Hittite Code" *prefers sentences which compensate victims for loss, rather than sentences which punish convicts for crime. It also regularly commutes death sentences to corporal punishment and reduces corporal punishment sentences to fines. To make these changes,* "The Hittite Code" *simply inserts* "Formerly, . . ." *at the beginning of the old law and then introduces the new law with* ". . . but now . . . ."

Parallels to "The Hittite Code" *in ancient Israel appear mainly in* "The Deuteronomic Code" *(Deut 12—26) and* "The Holiness Code" *(Lev 17—26). These parallels are especially clear in each code's use of similar technical terms. For example, the terms* "brother" *and* "brother-in-law" *identify citizens who have legal contracts with each other, rather than simply individuals who are kin to one another by birth. For example, in Deuteronomy 25:5-10, a* "brother-in-law" *is the executor of a will. The same legal connotations appear in the English use of* "sons" *in the title of a business, such as* "J.R. Everitt & Sons." *And although the terms* "sister" *and* "daughter," *which in English are used only to identify members of one's nuclear or extended family, in Semitic languages often carry important legal connotations as well. Another strong parallel appears in the practice of sealing a significant political or economic contract for the exchange of food and weapons by intermarriage.*

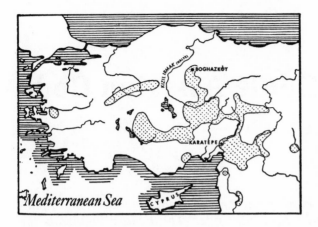

Fig. 35. **The map of Turkey shows areas where Hittite ruins have been found by the dotted design.**

Fig. 36. **A mother nursing her son. Perhaps the queen and crown prince. From Karatepe in southern Turkey.**

The most valuable women for such intermarriages are those mentioned in the twelve point decalogue in Leviticus 18:6–18.

Article 193

If a married man dies, then his brother must marry the widow; if his brother dies, then his father must marry her; if his father dies, then one of his brother's sons must marry the widow. No crime has been committed (Gen 38; Deut 25:5–10; Ruth 4).

Article 195

If a citizen sexually abuses his brother's wife while his brother is still alive, the sentence is death.

If a citizen, who is married to a woman who is also a citizen, sexually abuses his wife's daughter, the sentence is death.

If a citizen sexually abuses his mother-in-law or his sister-in-law, the sentence is death.

The Middle Assyrian Code

Tiglath-Pileser I, emperor of Assyria from 1115–1077 BCE, published "The Middle Assyrian Code." The treatise highlights the social concerns and interests of the Assyrian government during this period, especially its program of judicial reform aimed at clarifying definitions of legal guilt and responsibility. In 1903 German archaeologists found part of "The Middle Assyrian Code" at Ashur in Iraq. It was written in cuneiform on fifteen baked clay tablets.

Originally, "The Middle Assyrian Code" may have been four thousand lines long and probably followed the same literary pattern as "The Code of Hammurabi." An inspiring recitation of the military and political accomplishments of Tiglath-Pileser I introduces a major section of case laws.

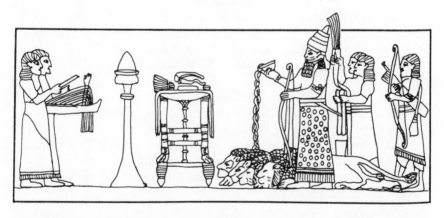

Fig. 37. **King Ashurbanipal pours a libation over the lions killed in a hunt. On the left, musicians play in front of the altar, and to the right the king's attendants wait.**

Parallels to "The Middle Assyrian Code" *in ancient Israel appear primarily in* "The Covenant Code" *(Exod 21—23),* "The Holiness Code" *(Lev 17—26) and* "The Deuteronomic Code" *(Deut 12—26).*

Article 8
If during a fight with a citizen, a woman ruptures one of his testicles, then the sentence is the amputation of one finger; however, if, even after medical treatment, his other testicle also ruptures, then the sentence is the blinding of both eyes (Deut 25:11-12).

Article 20
If one citizen has homosexual relations with another, then the sentence, following due process, is castration (Lev 20:13).

Article 47
If either a man or a woman prepares magical potions or objects and is caught with them in his or her possession, then the sentence, following due process, is death (Exod 22:18; Lev 20:27; 1 Sam 28:3).

The Book of Joshua

El Amarna Letters

The first 300 tablets containing The El Amarna Letters were found in 1887 by an Egyptian peasant woman, who sold them all for about one dollar. Eventually a total of 540 clay tablets were recovered and, so far, 378 have been published. El Amarna is the capital city which Pharaoh Akhenaton built about one hundred and fifty miles south of Cairo. They are diplomatic correspondence written to Pharaoh Amenophis III (1398–1361 BCE) and Pharaoh Akhenaton (1369–1353 BCE) by the governors they appointed in Palestine.

The letters describe a period during which the Pharaoh had little real control of Palestine. Some of these royal governors declare themselves independent of Egypt. Others join forces with a group known as The Habiru who pillage villages and raid trade caravans. Many of these letters sound the alarm, asking for troops to be sent to protect Egyptian interests, while others are written to defend the actions of the royal governors.

The letters were written by Canaanite and Egyptian scribes in a dialect of Akkadian using cuneiform script, but they include many Canaanite words and expressions. The El Amarna letters are the only inscriptions in cuneiform recovered in Egypt.

There is little linguistic or ethnic evidence for identifying The Habiru with The Hebrews. Nonetheless, these letters well describe the turbulent period in Palestine which is the background for The Books of Joshua and Judges.

Letter 244

To: Pharaoh, My Lord, My Sun
From: Biridiya, Governor of Megiddo

Your servant renews his oath of loyalty to Pharaoh by bowing to his feet seven times seven times.

Pharaoh should know that since he recalled his archers to *10*

Egypt, Labayu, Governor of Shechem, has not stopped raiding my
territory. We cannot shear our sheep, nor even leave the city for fear
of Labayu's soldiers. Because you have not replaced the archers,   *20*
Labayu is now strong enough to attack the city of Megiddo itself. If
Pharaoh does not see fit to reinforce the city, Labayu will capture it.   *30*
The people of Megiddo are already suffering from hunger and
disease.

I beg Pharaoh to send one hundred soldiers to protect Megiddo
from Labayu or he will certainly capture the city.

Letter 254

To: Pharaoh, My Lord, My Sun
From: Labayu, Governor of Shechem

Your servant, who is less than the dust under your feet, renews
his oath of loyalty to Pharaoh by bowing seven times seven times.

I have received Pharaoh's letter. Your fears are unfounded. I
am far too insignificant to be a threat to my Pharaoh's lands. I am
and always have been a faithful servant of Pharaoh. The proof that I   *10*

Fig. 38. **An Egyptian tomb drawing of typical men from Syria and Canaan, from where the Amarna letters originated.**

Fig. 39. **An Egyptian soldier with shield honoring the king.**

am neither a criminal nor a rebel can be seen in my regular pay-
ment of tribute and my willingness to obey all of the commands of
your provincial governor.

Despite the fact that wicked lies have been spoken against me,
my lord Pharaoh has not taken the time to look personally into my
case. The only crime that can be charged against me is that I invad-   *20*
ed Gezer. This is based, however, on the Pharaoh's confiscation of
my own lands. Milkilu has committed even worse offenses than I
have and no move has been made to take his possessions.

On another occasion, Pharaoh wrote me concerning my son. I   *30*
had no idea that he was consorting with The Habiru! I have since
handed him over to Addaya. Even if my lord wrote concerning my
wife, I would not withhold her. I would not even refuse to obey   *40*
Pharaoh's command to thrust a bronze dagger into my heart.

Letter 286

To: Pharaoh, My Lord,
From: Abdu-Heba

Your servant renews his oath of loyalty to Pharaoh by bowing
seven times seven times. What have I done to displease my lord
(Micah 6:3)? I have been unjustly slandered at the royal court with
the statement, "Abdu-Heba is disloyal." I am well aware that I
owe my position of authority to the mighty hand of Pharaoh, not
through inheritance from my parents. Therefore, why should I commit a crime against Pharaoh, My Lord?

Over and over I have told Pharaoh's chief adviser, "Why do you
support The Habiru and oppose me and the other governors?" It is
for my outspokenness that I have been accused of disloyalty! They
blame the loss of Pharaoh's lands on me, but the garrison, which
Pharaoh stationed here has been recalled by your adviser Yanhamu.
Thus we have no garrison to protect Pharaoh's lands. It is now
entirely up to Pharaoh to deal with this situation. Milkilu, Governor
of Gezer, has incited all of Pharaoh's lands to revolt.

On many occasions I have asked for an audience with Pharaoh,
but the hostility of Pharaoh's advisers has prevented me from receiving an appointment. Only if the Pharaoh sends a garrison to
protect his lands will I be able to come to court to speak with him. I
swear by the life of Pharaoh that the provincial governors are lost
and the lands of the Pharaoh are going to ruin. Not a single governor will remain in the Pharaoh's service.

May it please the Pharaoh to send the archers needed to reinforce the garrison. Facing no opposition, The Habiru boldly plun-

der the lands of Pharaoh. The only hope Pharaoh has to keep his lands under control is if archers are sent this year.
Attention: The Scribe of Pharaoh.

Be sure that at least this much of my message is brought to the immediate attention of Pharaoh, My Lord: "The lands of Pharaoh, My Lord, are going to ruin!"

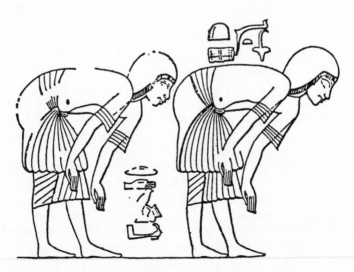

Fig. 40. **Officials of the royal harem bow before King Akenaton. From the tomb of Ramose at Thebes (19th century B.C.E.).**

The Stele of Merneptah

About 1208 BCE, Pharaoh Merneptah commissioned his scribes to prepare a hymn of victory celebrating his triumph over the Libyans in the fifth year of his reign. They used a stele (7 feet, 6 inches high) which had first been inscribed in Amenhotep III's time (1398–1361 BCE). Included at the end of this hymn is a poem recording similar victories over Asiatic people in Syria-Palestine.

The portion of the poem translated below contains the only mention of "Israel" yet discovered in Egyptian texts of this period. As a result, it has been used as one of the arguments for dating the Exodus and Conquest periods to the 13th–12th centuries. Since the Egyptian pharaohs often borrowed lists of conquests from older, well-known royal inscriptions, judgment on whether this is a valid argument must await additional evidence.

The princes who have opposed me now bow before me, saying: "Peace!" Not one raises his head in revolt. I have desolated Tehenu and quieted the land of the Hittites. I have plundered Canaan in a fierce manner and carried off spoil from the city of Ashkelon and captured the city of Gezer. The town of Yanoam in northern Canaan I have utterly destroyed, leaving it as if it had never existed. The people of the tribes of Israel have been laid waste, their offspring destroyed. Hurru—Canaan—has become a widow by Egypt's action! All of the lands there are now pacified; all those who were restless and rebellious have been bound into submission by the Pharaoh of Upper and Lower Egypt,—Ba-en-Ra Meri-Amon; the Son of Ra: Merneptah Hotep-hir-Maat, who is given life like Ra, The God of the Sun, every day.

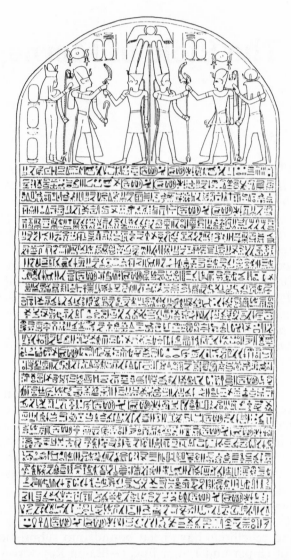

Fig. 41. **The Egyptian stele of the pharaoh Merneptah.**

The Book of Judges

The Story of Aqhat

Ugarit was an important commercial center on the northern coast of Syria, connecting the trade lanes between Egypt to the south, islands like Crete to the west and Mesopotamia to the east. Culture followed Ugarit's prosperity, especially between 1500–1250 BCE. Among this period's magnificent works of art and literature, recovered by a French excavation directed by C.A. Schaeffer during twenty-two seasons between 1929–1960, is "The Story of Aqhat." It is written on fifteen baked clay tablets in Ugaritic, a Semitic language like Hebrew. Ugaritic uses wedge shaped characters, but the characters represent individual sounds from an alphabet, rather than syllables, which was the earlier method used in Mesopotamian cuneiform writing and the hieroglyphics of Egypt as well.

In "The Story of Aqhat," tellers portray Aqhat, the main character, as the perfect son and perfect hunter. Danil, a king and a judge, is Aqhat's father, Danatiya is his mother, Paghat his sister. Danil and Danatiya were married a long time, but were unable to have a son until Ba'al, their divine patron, helped them conceive and give birth to Aqhat. Kothar-wa-Hasis, the divine armorer, makes the boy a unique and powerful bow and arrows. Jealous that Aqhat will not sell her his weapons, Anat, Goddess of Love and War, hires Yatpan, a soldier-of-fortune, to assassinate him. Paghat, Aqhat's sister, subsequently avenges his death.

"The Story of Aqhat" was very popular in the ancient Near East and in ancient Israel. For example, Anat's meeting with El and her plot to assassinate Aqhat are paralleled by the aftermath of Ishtar's meeting with Gilgamesh and her decision to assassinate Enkidu in Tablet Six of "The Story of Gilgamesh."

Likewise, the "barren-wife motif" in "The Story of Aqhat" appears in ancestor stories like Genesis 15:1–4, 16:1–15, 18:9–15, 25:21, 30:1–24 as well as in Judges 13:2–3, 1 Samuel 1:2–17 and 2 Kings 4:8–

17. In these stories, there is always a couple who want to, but cannot have a child. Yahweh intervenes to announce the impending birth of a child to the couple and tell them what to name it! Miraculous events highlight the birth of their child who is destined to deliver the people.

Finally, in Genesis 21:9–21, some of the episodes from "The Story of Aqhat" also appear. Here Ishmael plays Aqhat's role of the great hunter whose life is threatened by Sarah, playing the role of Anat, and whose life is saved by Hagar, who plays the role of Paghat. However, in Genesis 27, it is Esau who plays Aqhat the hunter, whose mother Rebekah—playing the role of Anat—tries to take away his inheritance.

"The Story of Aqhat" opens with Danil engaged in a seven-day ritual (Gen 1:1—2:4a; Neh 8:18) designed to appease the gods so that he and his wife, Danatiya, will be able to have a son and heir. For seven days, Danil feeds the gods at an elaborate banquet. Then, on the seventh day, Ba'al stands and addresses the god El, who is king of the gods in Ugarit.

(A.i)

Danil-the-powerful is sulking,
    He sighs for lack of a son like others have.   *20*
Surely he should have a son like his brothers have,
    —an heir like his relatives have!
He has blessed the gods with food
    He has filled their house with drink,
El, God of the Bull, bless him with a son,
    My Father, Our Father, fill his house with a child.
Put a son in his house,
    —an heir in his palace.
A son . . .
To erect a stele for his ancestral gods,
    To build a family shrine in the sanctuary.
A son . . .
To free Danil's spirit from death,
    To guard his footsteps from earth to underworld.
A son—Aqhat . . .
To enslave those who revolt against Danil,   *30*
    To drive away those who invade his father's land.
A son strong enough . . .
To take Danil's hand,
    —when he is drunk,

To put Danil's arm over his shoulder,
—when he is full of wine
(Gen 9:20–23; Isa 51:17–18).
A son . . .
To eat a funeral meal in the temple of Ba'al,
To offer a sacrifice in the house of El.
To patch Danil's roof when it leaks,
To wash Danil's clothes when they are dirty.

El agrees with Ba'al and dispatches a messenger to Danil with the promise of a son.

(A.ii)

Danil's face lit up,
His countenance shone.
He put his head back and laughed,   *10*
Put his feet up on his footstool and roared
(Gen 17:17).
He raised his voice,
He shouted:
"Now I can sit and rest,
my spirit can be at ease.
For a son like my brothers have will be born to me,
An heir like my relatives have. . . ."

For seven more days, Danil entertains the midwives of his court, who will assist him with the birth of his son. In Ugarit, midwives bear the same title as midwives in France, they are called "wise women"—"femmes sages."

Danil went home,
Danil entered his palace.
The midwives arrived,
The singers . . . ,
The chanters. . . .
Then,
Danil the powerful,
Danil the hero,
Danil the protégé of Harnam . . .
Roasted an ox for the midwives,   *30*
Threw a feast for the midwives.

Fig. 42. An Egyptian stringing the bow. From a tomb painting.

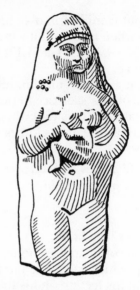

Fig. 43. A mother and child. From late Sumero-Akkadian times.

Wined the midwives,
    Dined the singers,
    . . . the chanters. . . .
Then, on the seventh day,
The midwives left his house,   40
    The singers. . . ,
    The chanters. . . .

At the carefully predetermined moment, the guests leave Danil and Danatiya and the couple have intercourse to conceive their child ". . . the joy of sex, . . . the bliss of bed." On this seventh day Danil starts to count the months until the birth of his son.

Parts of the tablet are missing, and the story picks up again in the middle of a speech by Kothar-wa-Hasis, the divine armorer. Kothar-wa-Hasis is talking about making a bow and arrows to give Danil for his son. Kothar-wa-Hasis finds Danil carrying out his duties as king and elder. Just as in the Hebrew Bible, "The Story of Aqhat" describes Danil sitting in the gate or on a threshing floor to pass judgment on the people (Judg 4:5; 2 Sam 15:2).

(A.v)

I will personally deliver the bow,
    I will present the arrows myself.
On the seventh day—
Danil-the-powerful sat at the gate (Gen 19:1; Ruth 4:1),
    —beneath a mighty tree (Judg 4:5),
    —on the threshing floor (1 Kgs 22:10).
Judging the widow's complaint,
    Hearing the orphans' case.
Danil looked up and out into the distance,   *10*
    And saw Kothar-wa-Hasis
    (Gen 18:2).
Running with giant strides,
    Carrying a bow and quiver of arrows.
Danil-the-powerful shouted,
    Called out to Danatiya his wife:
Prepare a lamb from the flock,
    Cook Kothar-wa-Hasis' favorite meal
    (Gen 18:6–7).
Kothar-wa-Hasis is hungry,
The Master Craftsman wants something to eat.

Aqhat uses his divine bow and arrows to become a mighty hunter (Gen 10:9; Gen 21:20–21). The goddess Anat envied his skill and wanted his bow, so she offered to buy it from the young hunter.

(A.vi)

Listen, Aqhat . . .
    Ask for silver and I'll give it to you,
    Ask for gold and it will be yours.
Just give me your bow,
    Let The Virgin Anat have your arrows.
No, Anat . . .   *20*
I will bring you . . .
    . . . yew trees from the Lebanon mountains,
    . . . sinews from wild oxen,
    . . . horns from mountain goats,
    . . . tendons from bulls' legs,
    . . . reeds from cane forests,
And you can give them to Kothar-wa-Hasis
He will build a bow for you,
    . . . arrows for The Virgin Anat.

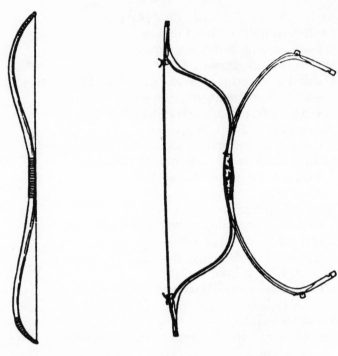

Fig. 44. **A double convex bow of a Semitic warrior. Egyptian painting of the 12th dynasty.**

Fig. 45. **A composition bow illustrating the strung and unstrung states.**

Listen, Aqhat . . .
Ask for perpetual life and I will give it to you,
   Immortality and I will grant it to you.
Your years will be as countless as Ba'al's,
   Your months like The Son of El.
Ba'al will bestow on you eternal life,   *30*
   Ba'al will feast you at his table.
Ba'al will give you immortal food,
   Ba'al will serve you the wine of everlasting life.
Ba'al will honor your name in endless song,
   The minstrel will sing your name forever.
No, Anat . . .
Don't lie to me, O Virgin,
   Don't waste your lies on men like me.
Can mortals become immortals,
   What becomes of mortals?

We are faces to be masked with plaster,
  We are skulls to be daubed with lime.
All mortals die,
  And death is my mortal end.
Furthermore,
My bow is the weapon of a man at war,   *40*
  Can it arm a woman on the prowl?
Anat roared,
  and exclaimed:
Listen to me, Aqhat,
  listen for your own good.
Your arrogance will cross my path again,
  Your presumption will lead you back to me.
I will overthrow you,
  I will trample you under my feet
  (Isa 10:6).
You darling,
You 'He-Man!'

Anat storms off to The Divine Assembly where she tries to get El to punish Aqhat. El refuses, but also agrees not to stand in Anat's way of getting revenge. So, Anat designs a plan to gain Aqhat's confidence so that she can murder him and take his bow.
  Anat sets her plan in motion by showing Aqhat a good place to hunt. Leaving him there to enjoy himself, she goes off and changes Yatpan, her accomplice, into a vulture. While Aqhat is field dressing one of his kills, Yatpan—now disguised as a vulture—approaches

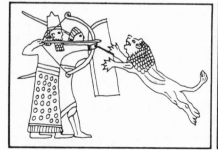

Fig. 46. **A hunting scene from the palace of King Ashurbanipal of Assyria, showing the king hunting lions. 7th century B.C.E.**

*him without arousing his suspicion (Gen 15:11). Swooping in be-
hind him, Yatpan changes back into a human, and stuns Aqhat
with a single blow to the head. He then murders him with three sur-
gically placed blows to the temple.*

*Once Aqhat is dead and the bow is hers, Anat weeps—not for
joy—but in remorse. She blames Aqhat for causing his own death
by refusing to give her the bow and arrows.*

*With Aqhat dead, there are no harvest rains. Ugarit's summer
crops wither from drought. Danil's daughter, Paghat, notices vultures circling over the palace.*

(C.i)

The vultures soar above the palace,   *32*
   The buzzards coast in the wind.
Deep within her heart Paghat weeps,
   Unnoticed she cries.
She tears the garment of Danil-the-powerful,
   She rends the robe of Danil-the-judge
   (Gen 38:34; Job 1:20).

*There is no public outburst of emotion by Paghat, whose feel-
ings are contained "deep within her heart." By tearing Danil's garment, Paghat officially files a gloomy economic forecast with the
head of state. Then, on the basis of her report, Danil revises his
administration's farm policies for the next seven or eight years.*

For seven years Ba'al will disappear,
   For eight the Rider of the Clouds will dispatch . . .
   (2 Sam 1:21; Ps 68:4; Ps 104:3).
. . . no dew,
   . . . no rain,
. . . not one flood,
   . . . not a single thunder shower
   (Gen 7:11; 2 Sam 1:21).

*Paghat saddles a donkey, and Danil, himself, rides off to survey
the drought damage (ii.50–iv.169). As he rides, Danil mourns the
death of his only son. He curses the murderer, and petitions Ba'al to
break the wings of the vultures circling the palace. One by one
Danil disembowels the crippled birds, searching for his son. The*

stomachs of the first two birds are empty, but inside the stomach of Samal, the vulture queen, Danil finds fat and bone of Aqhat. Danil buries the remains and places Abelim, Yatpan's hometown under interdict (Josh 6:26; Deut 21:1–9).

Just as Danil celebrated Aqhat's birth with the midwives for seven days, Danil laments his son's death with the mourners for seven years (iv:170–189; 2 Samuel 12:15–17). When the mourners leave the palace, Danil goes to the temple and eats the funeral meal for the son he had hoped would eat the funeral meal for him!

Paghat asks Danil to appoint her to avenge her brother's death (iv:190–209). Danil commissions Paghat by breathing into her nostrils the breath of life (Gen 2:7; Ezek 37:9).

(C.iv)

Bless me, Father
    And I will be blessed (Gen 27:38)   *194*
Choose me,
    And I will be chosen.
I will slay my brother's killer,
    I will destroy the ravager of my family.

Paghat bathes in the sea, before smearing her skin with blood-red dye and donning the uniform and knife of a warrior. Finally, Paghat disguises herself by wearing a woman's dress over her soldier's clothing.

First, she dons a warrior's clothes . . .   *205*
She thrusts a knife into her belt,
    She hangs a sword on her side.
. . . then, over all she puts on her woman's clothes!

At dusk, Paghat slips into Yatpan's camp. She asks to be taken to his tent, where she finds him drunk. Yatpan orders her to bring him more wine (Judg 4:19), as he brags about killing Aqhat. Coolly, Paghat ignores Yatpan and continues to get him more and more drunk (iv:210–224).

The end of the tablet is missing. However, there are two similar stories from the Hebrew Bible, which may suggest conclusions for The Story of Aqhat. "The Story of Jael" (Judg 4:17–22) recounts that ". . . as Sisera was lying fast asleep . . . Jael . . . took a tent peg and *hammer . . . and drove the peg into his temple. . . ." "The Story of* Judith" *tells how when Holofernes, ". . . was stretched out on his bed . . . overcome with wine . . . Judith went up to the bedpost, took down his sword . . . struck his neck twice with all her might, and severed his head from his body" (Judt 13:2 + 6 + 9).*

Fig. 47. **The image of the Canaanite goddess 'Anat standing on the back of a lion. She is naked and shows the symbols of a goddess of war and of love. Egyptian bas-relief. 19th Dynasty.**

The Diary of Wen-Amon

Throughout ancient history Egyptian envoys were sent to the Lebanon Mountains to harvest timber for architectural beams and carvings as well as for constructing the hulls and masts of ships. "The Diary of Wen-Amon" tells the story of one such envoy and the difficulties he faced. Wen-Amon traveled sometime between 1100–1050 BCE when Egypt was embroiled in domestic turmoil. Herihor, priest of Thebes in southern Egypt, and Smendes, ruler of Tanis in northern Egypt, were both trying to overthrow the titular government of Pharaoh Ramses XI. The princes of Syria took advantage of Egypt's weakness to drive hard bargains, by bullying Pharaoh's envoys. Wen-Amon is a typical bureaucrat, who is consumed with details. He seems almost unaware of how much times have changed, and naively employs outdated techniques in his negotiations with the Syrian princes, which are absolutely useless.

About 1899 archaeologists found this version of "The Diary of Wen-Amon" at el-Hibeh, Egypt. It was written on papyrus in colloquial Egyptian shortly after 1100 BCE.

There is no full parallel to "The Diary of Wen-Amon" in the Hebrew Bible, although it well describes the international power vacuum after 1100 BCE, which allowed a small independent state like biblical Israel to emerge about 1000 BCE. Furthermore, the text footnotes some interesting manners and customs which also appear in the Hebrew Bible. The use of threats by Wen-Amon is similar, although not nearly as effective, as those made by Rabshakeh, envoy of the Assyrian king, to the officials of Hezekiah in 2 Kings 18:13–37. Likewise, Wen-Amon carries his portable deity along with him and uses it just as Rachel uses Laban's teraphim (Gen 31:19–35). Ecstatic prophets appear in Byblos to advise the ruler just as they do in Israel. The cedars of Lebanon are considered herem or sacred property, just like the booty from Ai, and their misappropria-

95

tion demands the death penalty (Josh 7:20–21). Prince Tjeker Ba'al
harvests the cedars of Lebanon for Wen-Amon, just as Hiram of
Tyre does for David (1 Kgs 5:10–11). And Tanetne makes Wen-
Amon feel better by singing, just as David makes Saul feel better by
playing the lyre (1 Sam 16:14–18).

I, Wen-Amon, Elder of Amon's Temple Gate, was dispatched to buy timber for the river barque of Amon-Ra, King of the Gods. When I docked at Tanis, I presented my letters of introduction from Amon-Ra, King of the Gods, to Smendes and his wife, Tanet Amon, who ordered them read aloud. They agreed to do as Amon-Ra, King of the Gods, had commanded. I remained for the rest of that month in Tanis and then sailed in a ship under the command of Captain Mengebet.

When my ship docked at Dor, a city of the Tjeker people, Prince Beder welcomed me with a gift of fifty loaves of bread, a jug of wine and a side of ox. *110*

However, while we lay in port one of the ship's crew stole sixteen ounces of gold and ninety-eight ounces of silver in bullion and vessels, which I was supposed to use to pay for the timber!

I went straight to Prince Beder and reported: "I was robbed while at anchor in your harbor. As Prince of Dor it is your responsibility to investigate this crime and recover my money—money which came from Amon-Ra, King of the Gods, Lord of the Lands; and from Smendes and Herihor and other Egyptian officials; and from you and Weret and Mekmer and Prince Tjeker Ba'al of Byblos."

He replied: "Be careful whom you charge with a crime this serious. Do not bring your complaints to me! If the thief, who boarded your ship and stole your money, was my subject, I would reimburse you from my own treasury until the thief was apprehended. *120*
But since the thief was from your own ship's company, it is not my responsibility. However, give me a few days and I will see if we can find him for you."

So, I waited nine days in the harbor. Finally, I went back to Prince Beder. "Since you cannot find my money, at least let my ship sail." But he refused. "Settle down! If you ever expect me to find your money, you must stay here where I can contact you." However, I decided I could wait no longer and so worked my way up the coast to Tyre.

Eventually I left Tyre for Byblos, the city of Prince Tjeker Ba'al. In the harbor at Byblos there was a Tjeker freighter from Dor. I confiscated 101 ounces of silver bullion from the ship's owners and told them I would keep it until Prince Beder recovered my money or apprehended the thief who stole it. In the tent which I had pitched on the harbor shore, I celebrated my strategy for coming up with more money, which I hid in a statue of Amon, Patron of Travelers, which I had brought along to protect me on my journey (Gen 31: 19–35).

In reprisal for my actions, Prince Tjeker Ba'al of Byblos ordered me out of his harbor. I responded: "How shall I go? Are you going to pay for a ship to take me back to Egypt?" I spent twenty-nine days camped at the harbor of Byblos and everyday the Prince sent the same message: "Get out of my harbor!"

One day when Prince Tjeker Ba'al was offering sacrifice to his gods, a spirit possessed one of his servants, who became ecstatic (2 Kgs 3:15). The servant said: "Summon this Egyptian envoy and his statue of Amon, Patron of Travelers, who dispatched him to Syria." *140*

The prophecy occurred on the same night that I had located a freighter headed for Egypt. I had loaded my possessions on board and was only waiting for it to get dark, so that I could smuggle my statue of Amon, Patron of Travelers, on board.

At that moment the Harbor Master came to me and said: "Prince Tjeker Ba'al orders you to stay at anchor until tomorrow." I then replied: "Aren't you the same man who for the last twenty-nine days has ordered me to 'Get out of my harbor!'? You are only ordering me to stay overnight because you want me to miss my ship which is sailing tonight. Then you will come back in the morning and order me to move on!"

Fig. 48.　AMEN-RĒ͑

Fig. 49. **An Egyptian musician playing a harp. About 1000 B.C.E.**

The Harbor Master reported my objection to Prince Tjeker Ba'al who then ordered the captain of the freighter on which I had passage to remain at anchor until the next day.

The following morning Prince Tjeker Ba'al sent for me, but I left the statue in my tent by the harbor shore. As I entered, he was sitting in his upper chamber with his back to a window which overlooked the lapping waves of the Mediterranean, the Sea of Syria.   *150*

I greeted him with a blessing from Amon and he asked me: "How long has it been since you left the Temple of Amon in Egypt?"

I replied that I had been away from home five months. Then he said: "May I see your letters of introduction from Amon-Ra and his High Priest?"

I told him that I had given them to Smendes and his wife, Tanet Amon.

Prince Tjeker Ba'al became furious. "You have no papers! Where is the ship that Smendes gave you to transport the cedar timber and where is its Syrian crew? Is it not true that he plotted with the ship's captain to assassinate you and have your body thrown into the sea, so that there would be no trace of you or your statue of Amon, Patron of Travelers?"

But I objected: "Smendes outfitted me with an Egyptian,—not a Syrian—ship and crew."

But Prince Tjeker Ba'al was not convinced. "Why would Smendes send an Egyptian ship to Syria, when right now there are twenty Syrian ships in my harbor and there are another fifty Syrian freighters docked in the harbor of Prince Wekatara at Sidon under contract to him?"

(ii)

When I kept silent he went on: "What are you really doing   *1* here?"

I answered: "I am here to buy timber for the great and noble barque of Amon-Ra, King of the Gods. Therefore you should do what your father and grandfather before you have done."

Prince Tjeker Ba'al replied: "Yes, they did supply the timber. All you need do is pay me and I will also supply it. My predecessors did not carry out this commission until the pharaoh sent six freighters loaded with goods from Egypt and these items had been placed in their storehouses. Tell me now, what have you brought me?"

At that point he sent for a scroll from the time of his predecessors and ordered it read aloud. It was a receipt for various items   *210* valued at 950,000 ounces of silver!

Then he said: "If Pharaoh were my lord and if I were his faithful servant, he would not have to pay me a king's ransom in silver and gold—as he paid my father—to 'Carry out the commission of Amon!' In any case, I am not your servant, nor am I the servant of the one who sent you.

"I need only say the word and the heavens over the Lebanon Mountains will open and wash their logs to the shore of the sea. But where are the sails you need to power these freighters loaded with logs home to Egypt? Where are the ropes you need to lash them securely in place? . . .

"Amon is the creator of every land which hears the thunder of Seth Baal. Egypt, your land, was his first born. Only a fool would leave the land which invented ships and which discovered how to navigate to come all the way here to me."

I replied: "You are wrong! My mission is not foolish. All of the ships on the river belong to Amon. The Sea and The Lebanon Mountains are not Syria's but Amon's. He planted forests on The Lebanon Mountains as a source of timber to build the barque *Amon User He,* the greatest ship on earth. In fact, it was Amon-Ra, King of the Gods, himself, who ordered the High Priest Herihor to dispatch me on this mission with the statue of Amon, Patron of Travelers. But you have detained me and the statue of this great god for twenty-nine days in the harbor of Byblos. Surely, you knew Amon, the Patron of Travelers was there! He is as he always was and now would you bargain with him over the Lebanon? As for your statement that previous kings had sent gold and silver, that was because they lacked the ability to send life and health. It was in place of life and health that they sent these things to your predecessors. But Amon-Ra, King of the Gods, is the Lord of Life and Health, and it is he who was the lord of your predecessors. They made offerings to Amon throughout their reigns. You also are a servant of Amon. If you agree to carry out the commands of Amon, then he will bless you and your entire land with life and prosperity. If you refuse and withhold the timber which belongs to Amon-Ra, King of the Gods like a lion protecting its lair . . . (Josh 7:20–21)

Have your scribe brought before me so that I may send a letter to Smendes and his wife, Tanet Amon, whom Amon-Ra appointed to care for northern Egypt. They will provide all the sails and ropes you need to ship the timber. I will tell the scribe to write: "When I return to southern Egypt, I will repay you for everything."

A messenger took my letter to Egypt along with seven gifts: a keel, a bow-post, a stern-post, and four hewn timbers. The messenger returned from Egypt to Syria in the first month of winter. With

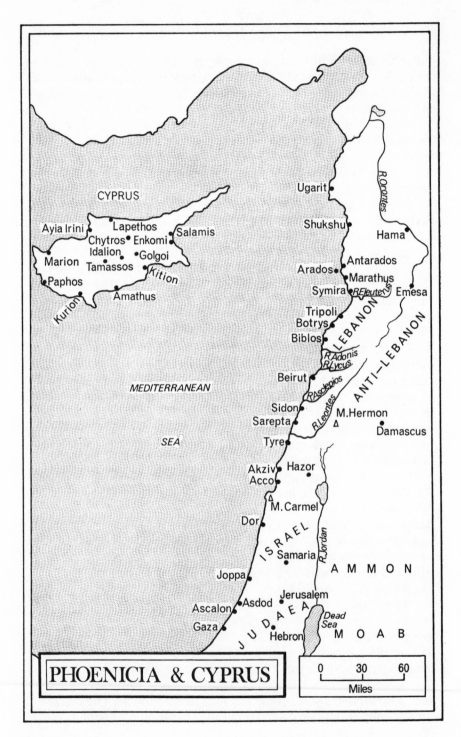

PHOENICIA & CYPRUS

Fig. 50.

him Smendes and his wife, Tanet Amon, sent Prince Tjeker Ba'al four priceless vases and one kakmen-vase, five silver vases, ten linen garments, ten bolts of linen fabric, five hundred smooth linen mats, five hundred ox-hides, five hundred ropes, twenty sacks of lentils, and thirty baskets of fish. In addition, Tanet Amon sent me personally: five fine linen garments, five bolts of fine linen fabric, a sack of lentils, and five baskets of fish.

Prince Tjeker Ba'al was delighted and immediately dispatched three hundred loggers with three hundred oxen and their supervisors to cut the timbers (1 Kgs 5:10–11). The trees were felled and lay on the ground through the winter. During the third month of summer the logs were dragged to the seashore.

Prince Tjeker Ba'al came out to inspect them and then said to me: "Come!" When I stepped forward, the shadow of The Prince's umbrella fell upon me and Pen Amon The Cupbearer shoved me aside, saying: "You are not worthy to bask in the shadow of Pharaoh's favorite son!" But this angered Prince Tjeker Ba'al who ordered The Cupbearer to leave me alone.

I was then formally presented to The Prince who announced: "I have carried out the commission which my predecessors had previously carried out. However, you have not done for me what your fathers had previously done for them. The final consignment of timber has now arrived and has been stacked. Obey my command. Load it and leave! Face bad weather at sea, before facing my bad *250* temper another day in port. You are lucky that I have not done to you what I did to the envoys of Khaemwase whom I detained seventeen years here in Syria until they died." At that point he directed The Cupbearer: "Take him to see their tombs!"

I pleaded, however, "Do not make me go see them. Khaemwase's envoys were merely humans, as was their master. You do not have before you only a man, though you say: 'Go see your fellow humans.' You should now rejoice and erect a stele with the inscription: 'Amon-Ra, King of the Gods, sent Amon, Patron of Travelers, his divine envoy, and Wen-Amon, his human envoy, to obtain timber for the great and noble barque of Amon-Ra, King of the Gods. I felled the trees and loaded it on board my own freighters worked by my own crews. I allowed them to return to Egypt so that they could request for me fifty more years of life from Amon.' Thus when another envoy comes from the land of Egypt who is skilled in writing and reads your name on the stele, you will drink from the fountain of life like the gods who dwell in the west." *260*

Then Prince Tjeker Ba'al said: "That was quite a long speech you have delivered." And I replied, "I can assure you that when I return to the Temple of Amon, The High Priest, upon seeing your accomplishments, will grant you merit for them."

I left Prince Tjeker Ba'al of Byblos and went down to the seashore where the logs were lying. However, eleven ships belonging to the Tjeker of Dor had docked there and they said: "Arrest him! Do not let his ship sail for Egypt!" I sat down right there and wept.

The scribe of Prince Tjeker Ba'al came to me and said: "What is it now?" and I told him: "The migratory birds have made their journey to Egypt twice. Watch them as they fly toward the land of cool waters! How long must I remain here? These men have come to arrest me?"

He went and reported everything to Prince Tjeker Ba'al and he wept also at this disagreeable turn of events. To comfort me he sent his scribe to me with two jugs of wine and a sheep. He also sent Tanetne, an Egyptian singer, who worked for him, with orders to: "Sing for him! Do not let his mind be troubled" (1 Sam 16:14–18). *270* He then sent word to me: "Eat, drink, and do not let your mind be troubled. I will make a decision on this tomorrow."

The next morning, Prince Tjeker Ba'al of Byblos convened his advisers to hear my case. He said to the Tjeker of Dor: "Why are you here?" They answered: "We have come in pursuit of the ships of our cursed enemy whom you are letting escape to Egypt."

But Prince Tjeker Ba'al instructed them: "I cannot arrest an envoy of Amon in my own country. I will send him away and you may then pursue and arrest him."

Then I was put on board my ship and sent away from that harbor. The winds carried me to Cyprus, The Land of Alasiya, where a mob tried to murder me. I fought my way through the crowd toward the palace of Princess Hatiba. As she walked from one building to

Fig. 51. **Egyptian ships. From a tomb painting at Beni Hasan.**

another, I got her attention and then asked those crowding around me if anyone spoke Egyptian. One person said he did and I asked him: "Tell My Lady that even as far away as Thebes, The Temple of Amon, Alasiya's reputation for justice is well known. Is she going to let an injustice like this ruin her country's reputation?"

Princess Hatiba asked: "What is he saying?" and I replied: "If a *280* raging sea and strong winds drive me to your land, will you allow me to be killed, despite the fact that I am an envoy of Amon? It is certain that a search will be made for me until the end of time. And as for this crew of Prince Tjeker Ba'al of Byblos, who are also in danger of being killed, surely he will find and kill ten crews of yours in revenge for their deaths."

Then she warned the people not to harm us and invited me to "Spend the night. . . ."

The Gezer Almanac

An important north-south trade lane—the Coast Highway—ran along the Mediterranean coast from Egypt to the Carmel mountains. An east-west cutoff connected that highway to Jerusalem. The ancient city of Gezer guarded the intersection. Here, around 925 BCE, a student practiced writing Hebrew on a piece of soft rectangular limestone about four inches long, four inches wide. R.A.S. Macalister recovered the text during his excavation in 1908.

The student copied an almanac identifying each month of the farmer's year with specific chores. In Syria-Palestine, the agricultural year begins in the fall, when olives are harvested and the October rains soften the sun dried soil enough to plant (Prov 20:4).

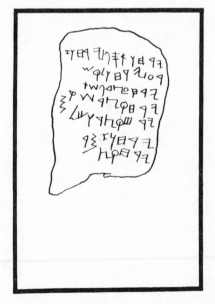

Fig. 52. **The Gezer Calendar, showing the archaic Hebrew script. Modern Hebrew uses Aramic script from the 6th century and later.**

104

It takes two months,   August–September
   to [olives] reap
   (Jer 40:10).
It takes two months,   October–November
   to [barley] sow
   (1 Kgs 19:19).
It takes two months,   December–January
   to sow [the wheat].
It takes one month,   February
   to pull [the flax]
   (Josh 2:6).
It takes two months,   March–April
   to [barley] reap
   (Ruth 2:23).
It takes one month,   April
   to reap [the wheat] and feast!
   (1 Sam 6:13; Isa 9:3).
It takes two months,   May–June
   [our vines] to prune
   (Isa 5:6; 18:5).
It takes one month,   July
   [summer fruit] to reap
   (Amos 8:1).

Fig. 53. **A scene of harvesting the grain (upper register), and plowing (lower register). Beni Hasan, tomb 3; 19th century B.C.E.**

The Books of Samuel
and Kings

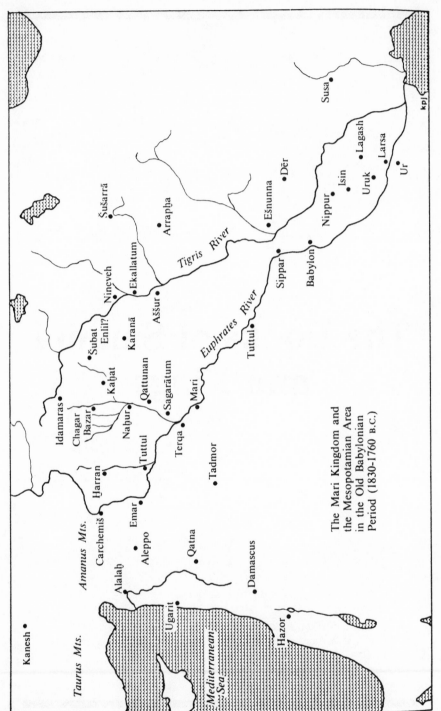

The Mari Kingdom and
the Mesopotamian Area
in the Old Babylonian
Period (1830-1760 B.C.)

Kanesh

Taurus Mts.

Amanus Mts.

Carchemiš

Alalaḫ

Ugarit

Mediterranean
Sea

Hazor

Aleppo

Emar

Ḥarran

Qatna

Damascus

Tuttul

Terqa

Tadmor

Idamaras

Chagar
Bazar

Naḥur

Kaḥat

Šubat
Enlil?

Nineveh

Ekallatum

Qaṭṭunan

Sagarātum

Mari

Karanā

Aššur

Tuttul

Šušarrā

Arrapḫa

Tigris River

Euphrates River

Sippar

Babylon

Ešnunna

Dēr

Nippur

Isin

Uruk

Lagash

Larsa

Ur

Susa

kpj

Fig. 54.

The Mari Prophecies

Between 1800–1750 BCE, Mari was a city-state that rivaled Babylon in its influence over the northern portions of Mesopotamia. It established alliances with several other city-states and maintained a network of communication between the royal palace and the provincial governors, which insured that King Zimri-Lim knew what was going on throughout the kingdom. Thousands of cuneiform tablets recovered from Tell Hariri since the 1930s mention prophets and their prophecies. These male and female prophets and their messages can be compared in style and language to the prophets in ancient Israel.

Some Mari prophets are called apilum *and seem to function as spokespersons for The Gods (A.2925). Some are called* assinu *and are temple personnel (ARM 10.7). Some are called* muhhu *and are ecstatic prophets. The personal names of the prophets never appear in their prophecies, which could indicate that Mari prophets were considered members of a sacred social class whose names could not be spoken (ARM 3.40).*

A.2925

To: Zimri-Lim, King of Mari
From: Nur-Sin, Official of the King of Mari.

Repeatedly I have written to the king about a gift of livestock to The God Addu—the sacred property which Addu, God of Kallassu, requests of you. . . .

The *apilum* prophet of Addu, God of Halab, said to me: "Am I not Addu, God of Halab, who has raised you (Hos 11:1) . . . who helped you regain your father's throne? I never ask too much of you. Respond to the appeals of your people when they experience injustice and give them a just verdict (Amos 5:15).

"You are to do what I ask and what I write to you to do. You will obey my word and keep watch over this land continually, as well as the country . . ." (1 Sam 12:14–15; 2 Sam 15:3–5).

ARM 13.23:1–15

To: Zimri-Lim, King of Mari
From: Mukannisum, Official of the King of Mari.

After I offered the sacrifice to Dagan for the king's health, the *apilum* prophet of Dagan in Tuttul rose and said: "O Babylon! What is this that you are continually doing? I will draw you up into a net. . . . I intend to give the houses of The Seven Allies, and all their property, to King Zimri-Lim.

ARM 10.7

To: Zimri-Lim, King of Mari
From: Shibtu, Queen of the King of Mari.

My lord: The palace is in good order. On the third day of the festival, The Prophet Shelibum fell into an ecstatic trance in the temple of The Goddess Annunitum (2 Kgs 3:15), who said: "O King Zimri-Lim, you will be tested by a revolt. Take special precautions. Surround yourself only with your most beloved and trustworthy officials. Let them stand continuous watch over you. Do not go out alone! I will hand over to you those who will test your rule." In confirmation of this, I am sending the king hair from the head of this *assinnu* prophet and cloth from the hem of her garment (1 Sam 24:5).

ARM 3.40:1–23

To: Zimri-Lim, King of Mari
From: Kibri-Dagan, Official of the King of Mari.

The favor of The Gods, Dagan and Ikrub-El, is continuous. The city of Terqa and the district are at peace. The same day that I sent this report to the king, the *muhhu* prophet of the god Dagan came to me and spoke as follows: "The God Dagan has sent me to you. It is imperative that you write to the king and ask that the funeral offering be made to the spirit of Yahdun-Lim, King Zimri-Lim's father." Thus I have written this message to the king. May the king take what he feels is the proper course of action (1 Sam 10:6; 2 Kgs 3:15).

Fig. 55. **Ebil-il, a Sumerian worshiper, praying. About 2500 B.C.E.**

Fig. 56. **Statue of the god Dagan. From the Sumerian period.**

The Stele of Mesha

Between 840-820 BCE, Mesha, king of Moab, commissioned a memorial celebrating the accomplishments of his administration. The memorial was carved on a curved topped, rectangular block of basalt three feet high and two feet wide. The thirty lines of text are written in the Moabite language using the Hebrew alphabet.

The Stele of Mesha was located in Dhiban, Jordan in 1868 by F.A. Klein, a German missionary. Subsequently, Charles Clermont-Ganneau (1846-1923), a French scholar, had a paper squeeze made of the inscription. Reacting to the attention the Europeans were

Fig. 57. **Ivory decoration in the form of a sphinx, from the time of King Omri in Samaria.**

112

giving their artifact, the local people heated the stele in a fire and
then smashed it into pieces with cold water. A third of the stele was
permanently destroyed. In 1870 the remains were restored by The
Louvre Museum, Paris.

   The inscription mentions Yahweh, the god of Israel; Omri, the
king of Israel and holy war (Hebrew: herem). Parallels to The Stele
of Mesha appear in Joshua 1–12, especially Joshua 6:17–21, 1 Kings
16:23–24 and 2 Kings 3:4.

   I am Mesha, King of Moab. My father reigned over Moab for
thirty years and I now reign after my father. Omri, the King of Israel,   *5*
controlled Moab for many years because Chemosh, our chief god,
was angry at his people. When Omri's son succeeded him, he
bragged that "I too will humble Moab." In my time, however, I have
triumphed over Omri's son causing Israel to be forced out of our
land forever! Omri and his son Ahab occupied our land for forty
years; but Chemosh dwells supreme there in my time. I built the city
of Baal-Meon and its reservoir, and I built the city of Qaryaten.   *10*
   Now the men of the Israelite tribe of Gad had always dwelt in
the land of Ataroth which borders our land, but I fought against that
town and I captured it. I slew all of the people of the town as a satis-
fying offering to Chemosh. I brought back from there Arel, its chief-
tain, [or perhaps a royal altar?] dragging him [it] before the god
Chemosh in the city of Kerioth, and I settled in that former Israelite
city (Ataroth) our own men of Sharon and Maharith.
   Then Chemosh said to me, "Go, take Nebo from Israel!" (Josh
8:1–17). So I went by night and fought against that city from daybreak until noon. I won a great victory and I slew the entire population of 7,000 men, women, and children—for I had promised the
god Ashtar-Chemosh that they would be devoted to him as a sacrifice (Josh 6:24; 8:24–27). I took the . . . of Yahweh, presenting it to
Chemosh.
   And the King of Israel had built Jahaz, and he dwelt there
while he was fighting against me, but my god Chemosh drove him
out before me (Josh 10:42). I recruited two hundred members of the   *20*
warrior nobility of Moab to take and then settle in Jahaz in order to
add it to my administrative district of Dibon.
   It was I who built Qarhoh, its gates and its towers, the King's
house and the reservoirs of water within the town. I also ordered the
people, "Let each of you make a cistern for himself in his house!" I

had Israelite captives cut the beams for the houses of Qarhoh. Then I built Aroer, and the highway in the Arnon valley and rebuilt the destroyed cities of Beth-bamoth and Bezer using fifty men from my loyal dependency of Dibon.

I reigned in peace over the one hundred towns which I had added to the land and Chemosh dwelt there in my time.

Fig. 58. **Painting of a fort defended from parapets and balconies. From Beni Hasan. About 1900 B.C.E.**

The Karatepe Inscription

This text is the longest known inscription in Phoenician. Other copies also exist written in Hittite hieroglyphic script. The Phoenician version has been found written on a large statue of Ba'al as well as on the body and pedestal of a gate lion. These inscriptions were found in the ruins of the city of Karatepe in Turkey, and date to the late 8th century BCE.

The text contains biographical material on Azitawada, the son and successor of King Awarik of Kue and Adana in Cilicia (southeastern Turkey). As an historical document, this text provides information on the management of the kingdom and the steps taken by the king to meet the needs of the people and to maintain relations with other kings. Its first-person style and assertion of accomplishment may also be compared to the Moabite Stone inscription which dates to the 9th century BCE.

Numerous parallels exist between this text and the Hebrew Bible. Its use of titles and conventional formulas, "from the rising of the sun to its setting," descriptions of cultic and economic activity, and the use of curses and blessings all are paralleled in biblical passages.

i

I am Azitawada. I am the steward of Ba'al and have been raised to my position of authority by [my father] Awarik, the king of the Adanites. With Ba'al's blessing I have become both father and mother to the Adanites (Isa 22:21), extending their territory from the rising of the sun to its setting (Isa 45:6; Mal 1:11).

In my time, they enjoyed all the good things of life, full storehouses (Gen 41:34–36, 47–49), and general prosperity. I filled the temple storehouses of Pa'r, and greatly increased the supplies of arms and the size of the army at the command of Ba'al and the gods. I dealt harshly with the criminal, expelling all the troublers of the kingdom. (Ps 101:8; Judg 19:22) I restored (10) the power of the ruling family, ensuring that an orderly succession took place and that proper diplomatic relations were maintained with other lands. My deeds caused me to be held in high esteem by other kings. My righteous and blameless actions were the outgrowth of my wisdom and my generous heart.

On all the frontiers of the land, I built strong fortresses to guard against the designs of those evil men (2 Sam 4:2) who had never served the house of Mopsos. Thus I, Azitawada, placed them under my feet and thereby allowed the Adanites to live in peace within the shelter of these fortresses (1 Kgs 9:15–20).

The lands to the west, which no man before me had conquered, I subdued. I, (20) Azitawada, subdued them and deported their population to the eastern frontiers. Adanites then settled

ii

(1) in their place, and in my day they dwelt there from the rising of the sun to its setting (2 Kgs 17:24).

In those places which had been without peace, where a man feared to walk abroad, in my day the woman was able to walk freely, twirling her spindles according to the command of Ba'al and the gods.

Thus in all my days the storehouses were full, life was good, and the Adanites dwelt without care or fear. At the command of Ba'al and Resheph of the he-goats, I built this city, (10) naming it Azitawadya. Its full storehouses, prosperity, and law and order provide protection to the Adanites of the plain and for the house of Mopsos. . . .

iii

I established the worship of Ba'al Krntrys in it and offered sacrifices for all the (1) molten images (Num 33:52). As an annual sacrifice, an ox was offered (1 Sam 1:21), and at the time of plowing and harvesting a sheep was sacrificed.

May Ba'al Krntrys* and the gods of the city bless Azitawada with many years of life, authority to rule, and strength beyond that of any king. And may this city and the people who dwell here possess full storehouses and wine (Prov 3:10), oxen and cattle in abundance. May they have many children (10) and in their strength of numbers become powerful. May they all serve Azitawada and the house of Mopsos according to the command of Ba'al and the gods.

*Krntrys: a non-Semitic place name, possibly Tarsus.

If (12) any king, prince, or man of renown removes the name of Azitawada from this gate [alternate version reads "from the statue of the god"] and puts his own name on it, or if in renovating the city he tears down this gate made by Azitawada and replaces it with a new gate containing his own name (Josh 6:26), whether with good or evil intent, may the lord of heaven and El, the possessor of the earth (Gen 14:19), and the eternal god of the sun, plus all of the children of the gods wipe out that kingdom and its ruler or

iv

(1) that man of renown. For only the name of Azitawada may endure forever, like the names of the sun and the moon (Ps 72:17).

Fig. 59. **Phoenician god standing on the back of a lion while holding a war club and lion cub. From Amrith.**

Fig. 60. **The Phoenician gate inscription from Karatepe in southern Turkey. 21 lines of script from a Hittite sculptor. 9th century B.C.E.**

The Annals of Shalmaneser III

After 1250 BCE, there were no world powers in the ancient Near East. The Greek, Hittite and Egyptian empires collapsed almost simultaneously. For the next five hundred years, small national states like Syria, Israel and Judah replaced the large multinational empires, but their political and economic power was limited.

The armies of Assyria crossed the Euphrates and campaigned west to the Mediterranean coast. But these were raids and hunting expeditions, not wars of conquest. Assyria's diplomatic and civil services were not prepared to administer an empire.

Shalmaneser III (858–824 BCE) recorded several military campaigns in his official annals. The Monolith Inscription describes his first campaign into Syria-Palestine during which he established a permanent Assyrian presence west of the Euphrates River with his victory at Qarqar on the Orontes River over Hadad-ezer of Syria, Ahab of Israel and their allies.

Parallels to The Annals of Shalmaneser III on The Monolith Inscription in ancient Israel appear in The Book of Kings (1 Kgs 16:29—22:40).

(ii)

Month of Airu
Day 14
The Year of Dain-Assur 78

I crossed the Euphrates for the second time using goat-skin boats since it was in flood stage. As I crossed into the region west of the Euphrates, I stopped at Ina-Ashur-utir-asbat, on the Sagur river, to collect tribute of gold, silver, copper, and copper vessels from several rulers. They were Sanagara of Carchemish, Kundashpi of

118

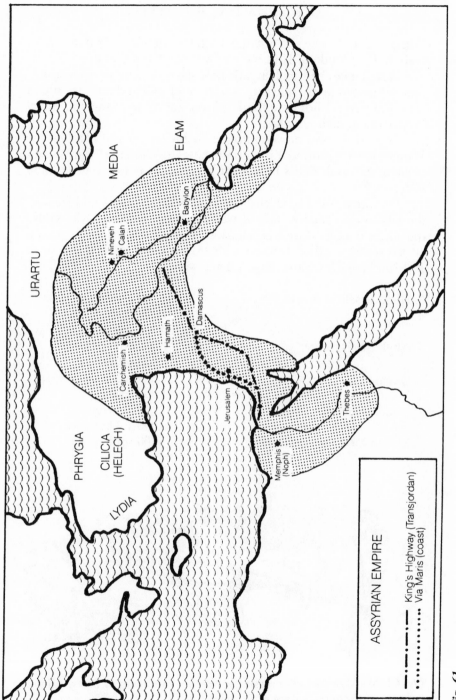

ASSYRIAN EMPIRE

– · – · King's Highway (Transjordan)
········· Via Maris (coast)

Fig. 61.

Commagene, Arame son of Guzi, Lalli the Melidean, Haiani son of Gabari, Kalparuda of Hattina, and Kalparuda of Gurgum.

Next I marched to Hamath (Aleppo). Fearing to oppose me, they submitted to my rule (lit., "seized my feet") and paid tribute in gold and silver. I honored them as new members of the empire by sacrificing to their god Adad.

Following this I moved into the hostile territory of Irhuleni the Hamathite. I captured his defiant cities of Adennu, Barga, and Argana and took rich spoils from his palaces before setting them afire.

Qarqar was the next obstacle in this campaign. I laid siege to the city and burned it once it was captured. Irhuleni, who could muster only seven hundred chariots, seven hundred cavalry, and 10,000 soldiers, allied himself with twelve kings against me (Josh 10:1–28; 11:1–12; 2 Sam 10:6–8). They were:

Hadad-ezer of Aram:	1,200 chariots
	1,200 cavalry
	20,000 soldiers
Ahab the Israelite:	2,000 chariots
	10,000 soldiers
Queans:	500 soldiers
Musreans:	1,000 soldiers
Irqanateans:	10 chariots
	10,000 soldiers
Matinuba'il the Arvadite:	200 soldiers

Fig. 62. **Assyrian soldiers crossing a river by swimming or using inflated goat skins. From the palace of Sennacherib.**

Usanateans:	200 soldiers
Adunu-ba'il the Shianean:	30 chariots
	xx soldiers
Gindibu the Arabian:	1,000 camels
Ba'sa, son of Ruhubi, the Ammonite:	xx soldiers

With the aid of my gods Ashur and Nergal (who goes before me), I routed these kings and slew 14,000 of their warriors with the sword. Like Adad, I rained destruction upon them (Josh 10:10–11). I covered the plain with their corpses (Ezek 37:1–2), and their blood flowed through the valleys of the land. Their dead were too many to bury (Jer 7:33), with bodies choking The Arantu (Orontes) River and corpses forming a bridge across its waters. I took as spoil their chariots and war horses (Josh 11:6–9).   *98*

The Black Obelisk
of Shalmaneser III

Among the leaders in Syria-Palestine who made use of Assyria's military assistance was Jehu, Israel's military commander. With Assyria's support, Jehu declared an armistice with Syria, formed a new government in Israel and abrogated its treaty with Judah. Shalmaneser III (859–824 BCE) ratified Assyria's treaty with Israel on a war memorial celebrating his fifth western campaign in 841 BCE.

The memorial is on a four-sided pillar of black limestone, six and a half feet high. There are five rows of inscription in bas relief, which reads horizontally from one panel to the other. Each row of panels is titled. The small stepped pyramid on the top of the obelisk and about one-third of the bottom are also inscribed.

In 1846 Austen Henry Layard (1817–1894) recovered The Black Obelisk of Shalmaneser III from Nimrud in Iraq. It is now in the British Museum in London.

Fig. 63. **Israelite tribute bearers carrying silver, gold, vessels, buckets and poles from Jehu, king of Israel to Shalmaneser III as a sign of homage. From the Black Obelisk.**

Fig. 64. The "Black Obelisk" of King Shalmaneser III recording his victories over other nations, including Israel.

Parallels to The Black Obelisk in ancient Israel appear in The Books of Kings (2 Kgs 9:1—10:33).

My sixteenth campaign west of the Euphrates took place eighteen years after I became Great King.

Hazael, king of Aram (Syria), ran for his life leaving 1,121 chariots, 470 horses and a supply convoy on the battlefield.

Iaua (Jehu), king of Israel, ransomed his life with silver, gold (i.e., bowls, vases, cups, pitchers), lead and hard wood (i.e., scepter wood, spear wood).

The Annals of Tiglath-Pileser III

It was an ambitious Assyrian politician named Pul, later crowned Emperor Tiglath-Pileser III (744–727 BCE), who formally inaugurated a new age of empires in the ancient Near East. He completely reorganized Assyria's bureaucracy to gain political and economic control of the trade routes running from the Mediterranean coast inland. Any embargo in these trade lanes cut off Assyria's imports of metals, lumber and horses, setting off riots among Assyria's citizens. Tiglath-Pileser III proposed that Assyria ratify three kinds of alliances with foreign governments. Assyria preferred to leave local governments in place rather than administer countries directly. Local entrepreneurs did a better job of managing commerce than Assyrian bureaucrats; local militia provoked fewer border incidents with Egypt than Assyrian troops.

Any government willing to align itself with Assyria's foreign policy and offer logistical and military assistance became an Assyrian satellite or ally. These allies retained self-determination in their domestic policies.

***Fig. 65.* Relief showing King Tiglath-Pileser III of Assyria who ruled from 745 to 728 B.C.E.**

125

Parallels to "The Annals of Calah-Nimrud" *in ancient Israel appear in* The Books of Kings *(2 Kgs 15:17–22).*

"I received subsidies from ... Commagene, ... Damascus, ... Samaria, ... Tyre, ... Byblos, ... Qu'e, ... Carchemish, ... Hamath, ... Sam'al, ... Tuna, ... Tuhana, ... Ishtunda, ... Hubishna, ... Arabia which included gold, silver, tin, iron, elephant-hide, ivory, linen garments embroidered with different colors, blue wool, purple wool, ebony, boxwood, luxury items (i.e., purple sheepskins, wild birds mounted with their wings extended and tinted blue) horses, mules, large cattle, small cattle and camels, some already bred."

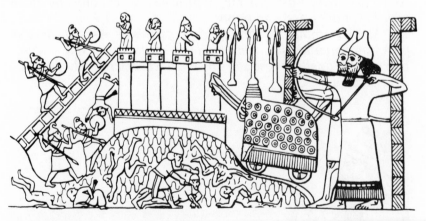

Fig. 66. **Siege of a town whose name is unknown by the Assyrian troops of Tiglath-Pileser III. The attack includes archers, spearmen and battering rams. Victims are impaled and beheaded. From the king's palace.**

The Annals of Sargon II

An ally of Assyria unable to meet its quotas, lost its self-determination and became an Assyrian vassal or colony. In a colony, officials
retained their titles and offices, but Assyrian personnel reviewed all
domestic policies to guarantee the colony would meet the empire's
military and financial budget. These officials functioned much like
officials of the International Monetary Fund function in the con-
temporary global economy. Their primary responsibility was to
design austerity measures for local governments to implement in
order to meet their debt obligations.

Only countries with healthy economies, efficient governments
and popular administrations managed to maintain their self-determination. Assyria's budget requirements increased continually, and
few local governments could meet Assyria's expectations and avoid
a taxpayers' revolt. Depositions and revolutions were frequent.

Any reticence or refusal on the part of local officials left an
Assyrian colony subject to outright foreclosure by Assyria. Assyria
would deport all government personnel, redistribute the colony's
population in developing regions of the empire and assign the

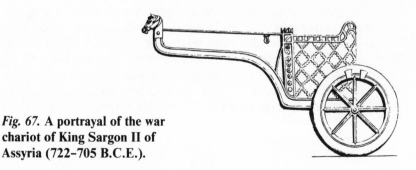

Fig. 67. **A portrayal of the war
chariot of King Sargon II of
Assyria (722–705 B.C.E.).**

colony an Assyrian military governor, incorporating it completely into the empire as a province.

"The Annals of Sargon II" chronicle the days of political and economic crisis when Israel went from the status of an Assyrian ally in 738 BCE, to an Assyrian colony in 732 BCE and finally to an Assyrian province in 721 BCE. Parallels to "The Annals of Sargon II" appear in 2 Kings 17:3–6.

Shalmaneser V (727–722 BCE) reduced the Israel of King Hoshea from the status of an ally of Assyria to its colony.

It is Sargon II (722–705 BCE), "the conqueror of Samaria," who converts Israel into an Assyrian province after King Hoshea signs a treaty with the pharaoh of Egypt and defaults on his tax payments to Assyria. It took Sargon II more than three years to win the war against the Bit Humria, "the land of Omri." Sargon II deported some of the population from Israel's capital city of Samaria to far-away places in the empire like "... Halah, ... the Habor, the river of Gozan, and the cities of the Medes (2 Kgs 17:6)." Others, he deported to nearby rural sections of Israel itself, and it is these people who become known as "Samaritans."

In the second year of my reign, Ilubi'di, a conspirator and an imposter to the throne of Hamath [Aleppo, Syria], signed a treaty with the cities of Arvad, Simirra, Damascus and Samaria and declared their independence from Assyria. Together they raised an army and attacked me. At the command of my god Assur, I—[Sargon II]—mustered an army and laid siege to his city of Qarqar. After I burned Qarqar to the ground and skinned Ilubi'di alive, the people of Arvad, Simirra, Damascus and Samaria assassinated their rulers and peace and harmony were once again established.

* * *

The governor of Samaria, in conspiracy with another king, defaulted on his taxes and declared Samaria's independence from Assyria. With the strength given me by the gods, I conquered them and took 27,280 prisoners of war along with their chariots. I conscripted enough prisoners to outfit two hundred groups of chariots. The rest were deported to Assyria. I rebuilt Samaria, bigger and better than before. I repopulated it with people from other countries I conquered. I appointed one of my officials over them, and made them Assyrian citizens.

* * *

I besieged and conquered Samaria, taking 27,290 prisoners of war. I conscripted enough from among them to outfit fifty groups of chariots. Subsequently, I rebuilt the city, repopulating it with people from other lands I conquered. I appointed a governor of my choosing, who reimposed the standard tribute payments.

Fig. 68. **Attack on the city of Gaza by troops of King Sargon II. The city stands on a mound, and the attackers have built a ramp to the right to bring battering rams against the gates. From Sargon's palace.**

The Siloam Inscription

"The Siloam Inscription" was discovered in 1880 on the wall of Hezekiah's Tunnel by children playing near its entrance into The Pool of Siloam in Jerusalem. The inscription is 19.5 inches wide and twenty-six inches long and was cut into the face of the rock wall of the tunnel. It is written in Hebrew, using cursive or longhand script. The first half of the inscription had been removed and is still missing, the rest is now in the Istanbul Museum, Turkey.

Hezekiah (715–687 BCE), king of Judah, commissioned the construction of this water conduit to secure Jerusalem's water sup-

Fig. 69. The Siloam inscription showing an enlargement of the archaic script in which Hezekiah's builders left their record of the water tunnel project.

130

ply in the event of an Assyrian attack on the city. It is unclear how the engineers laid out the route the diggers were to follow. However, the course of the tunnel indicates that the two teams were about to dig past one another before they made ninety degree turns and connected the two tunnels. The inscription describes these exciting moments. Water tunnels have been found at Gezer, Hazor and Megiddo, demonstrating that they were a common feature of a city's defenses.

Parallels to "The Siloam Inscription" appear in 2 Kings 20:20; 2 Chronicles 32:30.

... this is the story of how these two tunnels were joined together. The two teams working in opposite directions were digging toward one another with picks. The workers began shouting to each other when they realized they were four and one-half feet apart. Then, the teams turned toward one another following the sounds of their picks until they cut through the remaining rock and joined the tunnels. Thus, the water was able to flow through this tunnel one hundred fifty feet underground for some 1800 feet from the Gihon spring outside the city wall to the Siloam reservoir.

The Yavne-Yam Inscription

Little remains to us of Hebrew manuscripts and writings because most of them were written on perishable materials, such as papyrus or parchment. However, one nearly indestructible medium remains in fairly large quantities. Many short documents—lists, notations, letters—were written on broken pieces of pottery called ostraca. These potsherds were always at hand and messages could easily be scratched or written on them with ink. They give us a record of the development of Hebrew script and grammar and contain a wealth of personal names from the period of the monarchy, 10th–6th century BCE.

In the late 7th century BCE, a reaper sent a short message to the governor of the coastal region of Judah. This ostracon was found by archaeologists in the guardroom of the gate in a small fortress a short distance south of the site of Yavne-Yam. The letter was probably dictated to a professional scribe. It is written in cursive style and contains a formal address in the first two lines, which was a scribal standard (1 Sam 26:19). The reaper is asking the governor for the return of his garment which was unjustly taken from him by an official.

Fig. 70. **Typical Philistine pottery from the coastal plain of Palestine showing a bird looking backward. Yavne-Yam is located in this area.**

132

Let my lord the governor pay heed to the words of his servant! Your servant was reaping in Hasar-asam. The work went as usual and your servant completed his reaping and hauling before the others. Despite the fact that your servant had completed his work, Hoshaiahu son of Shobai came and took your servant's garment. All my fellow workers will testify, all those who work in the heat of the day will surely certify that I am not guilty of any breach of contract. Please intercede for me so that my garment will be returned and I will (as always) do my share of the work. The governor should see to it that the garment of your servant is returned and that no revenge be taken against your servant, that he not be fired (Exod 22:26–7; Amos 2:8).

The Lachish Letters

"The Lachish Letters" were written in Hebrew using a longhand or cursive script on twenty-one pieces of broken pottery or ostraca. The letters were composed with a reed pen and a black ink, generally manufactured by mixing soot with gallnut juice. The style of the prose is similar to that in The Books of Jeremiah and Kings, but there are several stock phrases as well as numerous misspellings.

Archaeologists recovered the letters in the ruins of a guardroom in the western gate of the city of Lachish at Tell ed-Duweir, Israel, where they were buried after the city was destroyed by the Babylonian army of Nebuchadnezzar in 587 BCE.

The letters mention persons who also appear in The Book of Jeremiah. They reflect the breakdown in military discipline and diplomatic protocol as Judah's military resistance to Babylon's invasion decays. The military commander in Jerusalem seems to be questioning whether or not his subordinate officer at Lachish is or is not cooperating with an unauthorized attempt by some members of the Jerusalem government to surrender to Egypt rather than Babylon.

Fig. 71 and 72. Front and back sides of the potsherd inscribed in black ink and found at Lachish at the time of the Babylonian destruction in 587 B.C.E. Letter #4.

134

Letter 3

To: Jaush, The Commanding Officer/Jerusalem
From: Hoshayahu, The Commanding Officer/Lachish—Your Servant.

May God bring tidings of peace to my lord!

I have received your letter, but I cannot understand my commander's question: "Did you not understand my orders?—Call a scribe and have him read them to you!"

I swear as God lives that I have no need of a scribe to read your orders for me! If one has come, I did not call him! I always take immediate action on those orders sent directly to me—do you think I would disobey a direct order?

I have received the following intelligence report:

"Coniah son of Elnathan, the commander of the army, has arrived on his way to Egypt and he has requisitioned . . . men and supplies . . . from Hodavyahu son of Ahijah."

With regard to the letter of Tobiah, Servant of the King, which was sent to Shallum, Son of Jaddua, by the prophet, saying "Beware!" I have already forwarded it to you (Jer 26:20–22).

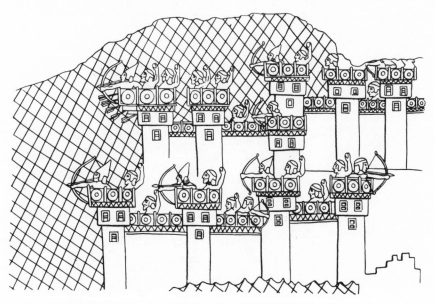

Fig. 73. **Portrayal of the defenders of Lachish found as a wall relief in the palace of Sennacherib of Assyria. About 701 B.C.E.**

Letter 4

To: The Commanding Officer/Jerusalem
From: The Commanding Officer/Lachish—Your Obedient
Servant.

May Yahweh bless you with a good day.

I have posted your orders in writing. Following your orders to make a reconnaissance of Beth-haraphid, I discovered that it had been abandoned. Semaiah has taken Semachiah into custody so that he can be transferred to Jerusalem for court-martial. I could not get him through the lines to Jerusalem today, but I will try again tomorrow morning. This letter certifies to The Commanding Officer/Jerusalem that I remain on duty to carry out your orders. Judah's signal fire at Lachish still burns, even after the [only other remaining] signal fire at Azekah has gone out! (Jer 34:6–7).

The Arad Ostraca

Like stagecoach stops and cavalry forts in the American West, fortresses like Ramoth-negeb (Josh 19:8; 1 Sam 30:27), which is probably Horvat 'Uzza, are located about every twenty miles on an east-west trade route connecting the King's Highway in the east with the Way of Sea in the west. This trade route is called the "Way to Edom (2 Kgs 3:20)" and is the main route leading to the Kingdom of Edom, southeast of Judah. The route descends from the vicinity of Arad to the northern end of Jebel Usdum range of mountains and from there to the Arabah valley of the Jordan River. Archaeologists have identified fortifications like Ramoth-negeb at both ends of the route. Because the construction plan of Ramoth-negeb is so similar to the installations at Kadesh Barnea, it is assumed that the route which Ramoth-negeb guards is as important as that which Kadesh Barnea guards.

The headquarters for the southeast sector of the Negeb is at Arad. The commander of Arad is responsible for the entire region and has to take care of the other fortresses in the vicinity with which he has daily communication. One military communique from Arad

Fig. 74. Ivory decoration from a Canaanite palace at Megiddo showing the victorious army bringing prisoners and booty before the king on his throne decorated with cherubim.

reflects a serious military emergency at Ramoth-negeb. The exploitation of the kingdom of Judah by both the empires of Egypt and Babylon so weakens Judah that the Kingdom of Edom invades Judah by crossing her southeast border in order to take control of the east-west trade route in the Arad sector. This Edomite invasion may or may not coordinate with the Babylonian invasion of Judah in 594 BCE (Jer 51:59).

Whether or not the troops from Arad and Kinah, which is Khirbert Taiyib, some 3.4 miles northeast of Arad, were successfully deployed at Ramoth-negeb, which is 5.6 miles southeast of Arad, is unclear. However, the destruction level at the Arad headquarters, where archaeologists found this communique, indicates that the Edomites overran the entire sector destroying not only Ramoth-negeb, but Arad as well!

. . . dispatch fifty soldiers from Arad and from Kinah . . . send them to Ramoth-negeb, under the command of Malkiyahu, The Son of Qerab-'ur, and he shall turn them over to Elisha, The Son of Jeremiah, in Ramoth-negeb, before anything happens to the city. You are to carry out these orders of The King of Judah under penalty of death. This is my last warning: Get those soldiers to Elisha before the armies of Edom attack!

The Annals of Sennacherib

As a result of the religious policies and moves toward political au-
tonomy by Hezekiah, King of Judah after 715 BCE, Sennacherib,
The Great King of Assyria (704–681 BCE), sent an army into Judah
in 701 BCE to put down the revolt. Sennacherib laid siege to Jerusa-
lem and devastated the surrounding countryside and nearby cities,
such as Lachish. "The Annals of Sennacherib" describe this expedi-
tion.

The first eight military campaigns are inscribed on a six-sided
clay prism. They are written in the Assyrian language using the
cuneiform script. Colonel R. Taylor recovered them in 1830 from
Nineveh at Nebi Yunus in today's Iraq. The Taylor Prism is now
part of the collection at the British Museum.

Parallels to "The Annals of Sennacherib" appear in 2 Kings
18—19.

(iii)

As for Hezekiah of Judah, he did not submit to my yoke, and I
laid siege to forty-six of his strong cities, walled forts, and to the   20
countless small villages in their vicinity, and conquered them using
earth ramps and battering rams. These siege engines were aided by
the use of foot soldiers who undermined the walls. I drove out of
these places 200,150 people—young and old, male and female,
horses, mules, donkeys, camels, large and small cattle beyond
counting and considered them as booty. I made Hezekiah a prisoner in Jerusalem, like a bird in a cage. I erected siege works to prevent
anyone escaping through the city gates. The towns in his territory   30
which I captured I gave to Mitinti, King of Ashdod, Padi, King of
Ekron, and Sillibel, King of Gaza. Thus I reduced his territory in
this campaign, and I also increased Hezekiah's annual tribute
payments.

Fig. 75. **Judean prisoners being led away to exile after the defeat of a city by the Assyrians.**

Hezekiah, who was overwhelmed by my terror-inspiring splendor, was deserted by his elite troops, which he had brought into Jerusalem, and was forced to send me 30 talents of gold, eight hundred talents of silver, precious stones, couches and chairs inlaid with ivory, elephant hides, ebony wood, box wood, and all kinds of valuable treasures, his daughters, concubines, and male and female musicians. He sent his personal messenger to deliver this tribute and bow down to me.

40

The Annals of Nebuchadnezzar II

"The Annals of Nebuchadnezzar II" of Babylon (605–562 BCE) contain summaries of military campaigns during his fourth through seventh years (601–598 BCE). During this time, Egypt and Babylon both claimed Syria-Palestine as their territory. Therefore, Nebuchadnezzar and his predecessors mounted yearly raids into the area as a way of maintaining their claim.

The Annals are inscribed in the Akkadian language in cuneiform script on baked clay tablets a little more than three inches high! The British Museum recovered the tablets from Babylon, about fifty-five miles south of Baghdad, Iraq today, and began publishing them in 1887.

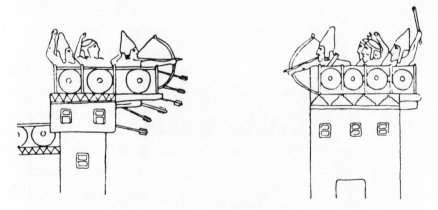

Fig. 76. **The citizens of Lachish fight off the attack of an enemy. Lachish was the second largest fortified city in Judah, and a prize for both Assyrian and Babylonian armies.**

As was the case with many kings of Mesopotamia, Nebuchad-nezzar uses the title "King of Akkad" as a way of tying his rule back into antiquity when the Akkadian kings, such as Sargon, ruled the area from 2400–2100 BCE. Nebuchadnezzar refers to the area where he and his army campaigned as "Hatti"—a name originally given to Syria-Palestine by the Egyptians. By Nebuchadnezzar's time this name was used by royal scribes throughout the Near East. His campaigns generally took place during December–January, the Babylo-nian month of Kislimu (Zech 7:1; Neh 1:1) or March–April, the Babylonian month of Adar (Ezra 6:15; Esth 3:7).

(v)

In his seventh year, 598 BCE, Nebuchadnezzar was forced to put down a revolt by king Jehoiakim of Judah. This event is also described in 1 Kings 24:1–17, although it is said to have taken place in the eighth year of his reign. Jehoiakim died during the siege and is succeeded by his son Jehoiachin. Nebuchadnezzar takes Jehoia-chin and a portion of the nobility and priestly class back to Babylon as hostages. He then appoints Jehoiakim's brother Mattaniah as the king of Jerusalem and changes his name to Zedekiah (Jer 37:1).

12

Fig. 77. **A Mushushu dragon from the walls of the city of Babylon at the time of Nebuchadnezzar. Glazed tile construction.**

Year 4

The king of Akkad marched his army uncontested into Hatti land. In the month of Kislimu (November) he led his army toward Egypt. When the king of Egypt heard of this, he sent out his own army. In the resulting battle heavy losses were inflicted on both sides. The king of Akkad then returned with his army to Babylon.

Year 5

The king of Akkad stayed in his own country organizing his chariots and horses.

Year 6
Month of Kislimu

The king of Akkad moved his army into Hatti land. They raided the desert area taking a great deal of booty from the herds of the Arabs and their sacred images. The king returned to his country in the month of Addaru (February).

Year 7
Month of Kislimu

The king of Akkad moved his army into Hatti land. He laid siege to the city of Judah (2 Kgs 24:10) and the king took the city on the second day of the month of Addaru. He appointed a new king to his liking (2 Kgs 24:17) and carried away great amounts of booty from the city to Babylon (2 Kgs 24:13-16).

The Books of Ezra
and Nehemiah

The Cylinder of Cyrus

"The Cylinder of Cyrus," dated to ca. 538 BCE, established a policy of the Persian government of returning hostage peoples to their homelands and restoring the temples of their gods. It had been standard procedure during the reign of Nebuchadnezzar of Babylon and his successor, Nabonidus, to hold portions of the population of vassal states as hostages in and around Babylon. The people of Judah had experienced two deportations of this type in 597 BCE and again in 587-586 BCE following their failed revolts against Babylon (2 Kgs 24-25 and Jer 34:1-7). When Cyrus of Persia captured Babylon in 540 BCE, he decided that more revolts could be prevented by allowing hostages to return home, if they wished, and providing funds needed to rebuild their temples (Ezra 1:1-4; 6:3-5).

The Decree of Cyrus was inscribed in Akkadian using cuneiform script on a baked cylinder about nine inches long. Few Persians understood Akkadian, but it was the official language in which all formal documents were published. Hormuzd Rassam (1826-1910) recovered The Cylinder of Cyrus for The British Museum from Ashurbanipal's library at Nineveh.

The Book of Isaiah (Isa 45:1) gives Cyrus the title of "The Anointed" or "The Messiah." He is the only non-Jew to be given such an honor. No doubt, his decision to allow the Jews in Babylon to return to Judah earned him this title in biblical tradition.

The temple in Jerusalem, which Cyrus authorizes, will not actually be rebuilt until ca. 515 BCE during the reign of Darius, his successor. The Book of Ezra (Ezra 6:1-15) describes how Darius searched the royal archives for The Decree of Cyrus. The scroll which Darius found may well have been a copy of The Cylinder inscription.

The first portion of the inscription on The Cylinder is a list of charges against King Nabonidus of Babylon, whom Cyrus defeated.

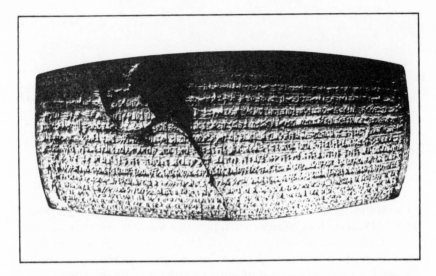

Fig. 78. **The inscription of Cyrus the Great of Persia written on a cylinder-shaped clay surface.**

They center around his improper prayers and sacrifices and his tyrannical practices.

The worship of Marduk, The King of The Gods in Babylon, Nabonidus made into an abomination. . . . He tormented Babylon's people with the yoke of forced labor (1 Kgs 12:4), never giving them any relief. Because of the complaints of the people, Marduk, The Lord of The Gods, became angry, departing the region along with The Gods whose statues had been moved to Babylon. Marduk . . . searched through all the countries for a righteous ruler willing to lead him in the annual procession. He spoke the name of Cyrus, King of Anshan, declaring him Ruler of All the World. . . . Marduk, The Great Lord and Protector of his People, looked with pleasure at Cyrus' good deeds and upright heart. Thus, Marduk ordered Cyrus to march against his city of Babylon. He marched with Cyrus as a friend while the army strolled along without fear of attack. Marduk allowed Cyrus to enter Babylon without a battle . . . and delivered Nabonidus, the king who did not worship him, into Cyrus' hands.

Cyrus is "welcomed" by the princes and governors of the city. They bow down to Cyrus and his son and heir, Cambyses. The

Cylinder of Cyrus then takes up the commentary of his victory and its aftermath, describing how he became the worshipper and servant of all of the gods.

When I entered Babylon as a friend and established my seat of government there in the palace of the king, Marduk caused the people to love me and I worshipped him daily. My troops kept order in the streets of Babylon and throughout the land of Sumer and Akkad. In Babylon I ended the practice of forced labor and helped rebuild their ruined houses.

All the kings of the entire world, from the Upper to the Lower Sea, those seated in throne rooms, or other types of dwellings as well as the tent dwellers from the land in The West, brought me tribute and kissed my feet in Babylon.

To all the regions, as far as Ashur and Susa, Agade, Eshnunna, the towns of Zamban, Me-Turnu, Der and the region of the Gutians, I returned the images of their gods to their sanctuaries which had been in ruins for a long period of time. I now established for them

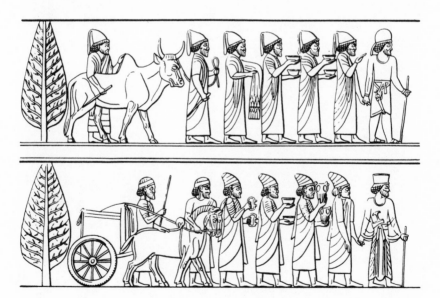

Fig. 79. **Babylonians and Persians bringing tribute before the Persian King Xerxes.**

permanent sanctuaries. I also gathered all the former inhabitants of these places and returned them to their homes.

Furthermore, upon the command of Marduk, I resettled all The Gods of Sumer and Akkad, which Nabonidus had moved to Babylon, unharmed in their former places to make them happy . . . and I endeavored to repair their dwelling places.

The Book of Psalms

The Hymn to the Aton

"The Hymn to the Aton" *was inscribed in Egyptian hieroglyphics on the wall of The Tomb of Eye, which Pharaoh Akhenaton (1365–1348 BCE) built for Queen Nefertiti's father at Tell el-Amarna. The Egypt Exploration Fund excavated the site in 1891 and the German Orientgesellschaft continued the work from 1911–1914.*

The hymn contains some lines from older hymns celebrating The Aton, The Sun Disc, and some conventional literary formulas typical of the genre. However, Akhenaton emphasized the exclusive worship of The Aton and his son, The Pharaoh. Akhenaton's religious reform cannot be called "monotheism," because The Aton and The Pharaoh are divine and, furthermore, The Aton is a combination of gods like Ra, Har-of-the-Horizon and Shu.

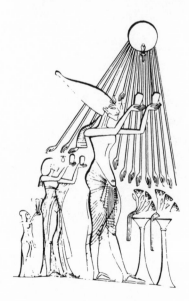

Fig. 80. **King Akhenaton with his wife and daughters worshiping the sun disk, the Aton, who extends life giving rays, pictured as hands.**

153

Interestingly, at one point, the hymn celebrates The Aton for doing everything a good midwife does for her mothers and their children. Both work with a man's "seed" and a woman's "fluid;" advise expectant mothers on proper nutrition; soothe the agitated fetus during midterm traumas; clear the airway of the newborn; and supply everything else the newborn needs.

There are several close parallels to "The Hymn to The Aton" in The Book of Psalms (Ps 104; 139).

As you rise over the horizon, O Aton, First Among The Gods
   Your beauty is made manifest, O Giver of Life.
You rise in the east
   You fill every land with beauty.
Your glory shines high above every land,
   Your rays enrich all the lands you created.
O Ra, you reach to the ends of the earth,
   You bestow them on Akhenaton, your beloved son.
Although you are far away,
   Your rays touch the earth.
Although you shine on every human face,
   No one sees you go.
When you set upon the western horizon,
   The earth lies in darkness and death.
Sleepers lie beneath their covers,
   Seeing no one around them.
Their pillows could vanish,
   They would not even notice.
The lion leaves his cave,
   The serpent strikes,
   The darkness blankets the land
   (Ps 104:20–21).
The lands lie silent,
   He who made them rests on the horizon.
At daybreak, you rise again over the horizon,
   You shine as The Aton bringing day.
Your rays chase away the darkness,
   The Two Lands of Egypt rejoice (Ps 104:22–23)!
Awake and erect,
   You raise them up.
Bathed and dressed,
   They raise their hands in praise.
The whole land goes to work. . . ,

Cattle graze contented,
    Trees and plants turn green.
Birds fly to their nests (Ps 104:11-14),
    They spread their wings to praise your Ka.
All things come to life,
    When you have risen.
Ships and barges sail up and down,
    Canals open at your rising.
Fish swim the river (Ps 104:25-26),
    Your rays penetrate even dark waters.
O Lord, our Lord, how majestic is your name (Ps 8:1),
    You join a woman and a man,
You form the fetus in its mother's womb (Ps 139:13),
    You soothe the crying child unborn,
You nurse the hungry infant in the womb,
    You breathe into its nostrils the breath of life
    (Gen 2:7).
You open the newborn's mouth on the day of its birth
    You meet every human need.

. . . .

In Khor [Syria-Palestine], Kush and Egypt,
    You assign each a place.
You allot to each both needs and food,
    You count out to each the days of life
    (Ps 104:27).

. . . .

You made the heavens in which to rise,
    That you might observe all things.
You alone are The Aton (Ps 104:24),
    Yet you alone rise—The Source of Life.
You alone are so far away,
    . . . and yet so near.
Your manifestations are numberless
    You are The Aton, The Source of Life.
Every town, harbor, field, road and river sees your light,
    . . . feels your warmth.
You are The Aton,
    You are The Daylight of The Earth.
. . . You are my desire,
    No one knows you except Akhenaton, your son.
You have revealed yourself to me,
    You have shown me your plans and your power.

Your hand made The Earth,
 You created it.
When you rise,
 The Earth lives.
When you set,
 The Earth dies (Ps 104:29–30).
You are Life itself,
 All live through you.
Every eye sees clearly until you set,
 All work must wait until you rise again.
At your rising, every arm works for The Pharaoh,
 At your creation, every foot sets off to work.
You raise up the people for the son of your body,
 . . . for The Pharaoh of Upper and Lower Egypt,
Who rules with the spirit of Maat, The God of Truth,
 . . . Akhenaton and her royal highness, Nefertiti.

Fig. 81. **An Egyptian noble hunts birds in the Nile marshes and papyrus thickets. Beni Hasan tomb 3. 19th century B.C.E.**

The Stories of Ba'al and Anat

"The Stories of Ba'al and Anat" *are preserved on six broken clay tablets from Ugarit. These versions of the stories were written in the Ugaritic language in the cuneiform script about 1400 BCE. The tablets were recovered along with hundreds of others by a French team headed by Claude F.A. Schaeffer (1898–1982), which dug at Ras Shamra, Syria, between 1929–1939 and after 1950. Hans Bauer (1878–1937) pioneered the translation of Ugaritic, an alphabetic language with thirty-two letters.*

Because much of the text of "The Stories of Ba'al and Anat" *is fragmentary, it is impossible to tell the exact order of the stories or their original purpose. Perhaps the stories were told during seasonal festivals at Ugarit. For example, on New Year's eve, the people of Ugarit celebrated a festival to mourn the death of Ba'al during the dry season which was ending (Ezek 8:14), and his resurrection to life during the rainy season which was just beginning.*

The following selections from "The Story of Ba'al and Anat" *reflect the power and place of Ba'al and Anat in Ugarit's Divine Assembly.*

Parallels to "The Stories of Ba'al and Anat" *appear primarily in* The Book of Psalms.

Anat Goes to War
(I.ii)

Anat locked the doors of her house,
  Joined her troops at the foot of the mountain.
Then Anat waged a fierce battle on the plain,
  Slaughtered the armies of two cities.

157

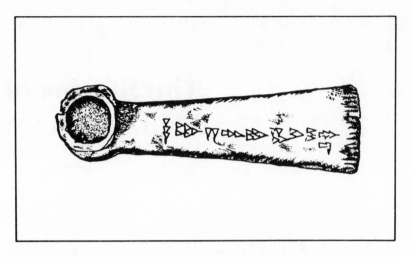

***Fig. 82.* An axe head from Ugarit with a cueniform inscription on it.**

She vanquished the warriors from the sea coast in the west,
   Destroyed the warriors from the east.
Their heads lay like clods of soil under her feet,
   Their hands matted like locusts in a swarm around her   *10*
   (Judg 7:12).
She strung their heads to make a necklace,
   She wove their hands to make a belt.
She waded up to her knees in warriors' blood,
   Up to her thighs in their guts (Isa 63:3–6).
With her spear she routed seasoned warriors,
   With her bow she turned back veterans of many wars.
Then, Anat went back to her house,
   The goddess returned to her palace.
But the fierce battle on the plain was not enough for her,
   With the slaughter of two armies, she was not content.   *20*
So, she built bleachers for soldiers,
   Set up tables for warriors,
   ... thrones for heroes.
Once again, Anat could fight with vigor,
   Slaughter everyone in sight.
Anat's body trembled with gladness,
   Her heart filled with joy (Ps 16:9),
   Her soul gloated with triumph,

As, again, she waded knee deep in warriors' blood,
  Up to her thighs in their guts.
Until, finally, these deadly games were enough for her,
  With the slaughter in her arena, she was content. *30*
The warriors' blood was washed from her house,
  The oil of peace was poured from a bowl.
The Virgin Anat washed her hands,
  Anat, Queen of All Nations, cleaned her nails
  (Exod 19:10).
She washed the warrior's blood from her hands,
  . . . their guts from her nails.
She dismantled the bleachers,
  Put the tables away,
  Took down the thrones.
She washed herself with dew from the sky,
  She anointed herself with oil from the earth,
She bathed with rain from The Cloud Rider (Ps 68:4; 104:3)
  With dew from the sky,
  With moisture from the stars.

Ba'al Builds A House
(I.iv)

Unlike other gods, Ba'al does not have a house of his own (2 Sam 7:1-17; 1 Kgs 5:3-6; 1 Chron 17:1-14). He shares The House of El along with the female gods of rain and fertility. When he complains about these arrangements, Anat intercedes with El for him.

Ba'al complained to Anat:
. . . .
"I have no house like other gods,
  No temple like the other Sons of Asherah!
"I must stay on in The House of El, my father,
  . . . lodge in The House of Unmarried Women!
"With Asherah, Goddess of the Sea,
  And Pidray, Goddess of Dew, *50*
"With Tallay, Goddess of Rain,
  And Arsay, Goddess of The Waters."
Anat then swears to Ba'al:
"El, God of the Bull, will listen to me (Zech 1:3),
  I will make sure that he answers me.
"I shall lead him like a lamb to slaughter (Jer 11:19),
  I shall cover his old grey head with blood (1 Kgs 2:9),

Fig. 83. The god Baal shown as god of the storm with the lightning spear and thunder club.

Fig. 84. Ugaritic plaque with a female fertility deity feeding male stags or goats.

. . . fill his old grey beard with guts (Isa 46:4) . . .
". . . if he does not give Ba'al a house like the other gods,
a temple like the other Sons of Asherah!"

(I.v)

She stamped her foot and the earth trembled,   5
  She headed straight for El,
She journeyed to The Source of The Twin Rivers (Ps 29:10),
  . . . to The Fountain of The Twin Waters (Job 38:16).
She walked right into El's Royal Compound,
  Burst into The Tent of The King, The Father of Time.
. . . .
Then, The Virgin Anat spoke:
"El, how can you rejoice with your sons,   20
  or celebrate with your daughters?
"How dare anyone in your palace be happy!
. . . .

I am going to smash your skull,
   cover your old grey head with blood,
   fill his old grey beard with guts."
From The Seven Pillars of Wisdom (Prov 9:1),
   From The Eight Halls of Judgment (Eccl 11:2) . . .
El spoke:
"My daughter, you are a warrior,
   No other goddess surpasses your ferocity!
"Tell me, Anat, my virgin daughter,
   What do you want me to do?"
The Virgin Anat answered:
"El, your decrees are wise.
   Your wisdom endures forever!   *30*
   Happy the life which you command!
"But mighty Ba'al is Our King (Ps 95:3; 96:4; 97:9),
   Ba'al is Our Judge Unsurpassed.
"All of us must bear his chalice,
   All of us must hand him the cup!"
Then she shouted at El, God of the Bull,
   Screamed at El, The King, her creator;
Cried out against Asherah and her sons,
   . . . against the Goddess and her whole family:
"Ba'al has no house like the other gods,
   No temple like the other Sons of Asherah!"

By this combination of threats and flattery, Anat convinces El that Ba'al must have his own temple. El orders Kothar-wa-Hasis, The Divine Craftsman, to build The House of Ba'al.

Ba'al Battles Yam
(III.i)

Other gods, especially Yam The Sea and Nahar, The River of Judgment, dispute Ba'al's right to a house. A battle pitting Ba'al The Storm against Yam The Sea and Nahar, The River of Judgment, then begins.

Yam The Sea sent messengers to The Divine Assembly,
   Nahar, The River of Judgment, dispatched envoys. . . .
The envoys departed at once,
   they did not delay.
They went straight to The Mountain of El,   *20*
   . . . to The Divine Assembly.

The Gods were eating,
   The Holy Ones were right in the middle of dinner.
   Ba'al stood beside El.
When The Gods saw them coming,
   . . . caught sight of the messengers of Yam,
   —the envoys from Nahar The River of Judgment,
They put their heads on their knees (1 Kgs 18:42),
   —down on the seats of their divine thrones.
But Ba'al rebuked them:
"Why put your heads on your knees,
   . . . down on the seats of your divine thrones?
"Do not be afraid of the messengers of Yam,
   —the envoys from Nahar The River of Judgment.
"Lift your heads up off your knees (Ps 24:9),
   Raise your heads from the seats of your divine thrones.
"I will speak to the messengers of Yam for you,
   —the envoys from Nahar, The River of Judgment."
The Gods lifted their heads from their knees,
   Raised their heads from their divine thrones.
When the messengers of Yam arrived,   *30*
   —the envoys of Nahar, The River of Judgment,
They did not bow before El,
   They did not prostrate before The Divine Assembly.
. . . .
They said to El, God of the Bull,
   . . . Father of Yam:
"Hear the word of Yam The Lord,
   —our master, Nahar, The River of Judgment:
"El must extradite the one in custody,
   . . . he whom The Divine Assembly is protecting.   *35*
"Surrender Ba'al and his followers,
   The Son of Dagan, whose power I will inherit."
El, God of the Bull,
   . . . Father of Yam answered:
"Ba'al is your slave, O Yam,
   Ba'al is your slave, O Nahar,
   The Son of Dagan is your prisoner.
"He will be turned over to you as a gift from The Gods,
   . . . as a present from The Holy Ones."

Ba'al becomes so angry, that he takes out his battle-ax and is
about to kill the envoys when Asherah reminds him that messen-

gers enjoy diplomatic immunity and cannot be killed because of the message they deliver (Jer 26:16–19). The text breaks off at this point.

By piecing together the remaining fragments, it seems that Yam drives Ba'al off Mt. Zaphon, and then tries to get permission to build a house of his own. However, Athtaru, The God of Irrigation, argues that Yam should not have a house because he has no wife. Yam counters by demanding that El give him both a wife and a house!

Finally, with the help of Kothar-wa-Hasis, Ba'al intervenes and resolves the case.

Kothar-wa-Hasis said:
    "Listen to me, Almighty Ba'al,
    Hear me out, Rider of the Clouds,

(III.iv)
"Now is the time for you to strike,
    Now is the time for you to slay your enemies,   *10*
    . . . to eliminate your rivals.
    . . . to establish your kingship forever (2 Sam 7:13)
    . . . your domain into eternity" (Ps 145:13).
Then, Kothar-wa-Hasis forged a battle-ax,
    and christened it: "Chaser!"
"Chase Yam away,
    chase Yam from his throne,
    . . . Nahar from his seat of power!
"Fly from the hand of Ba'al,
    Fly like an eagle from his fingers!

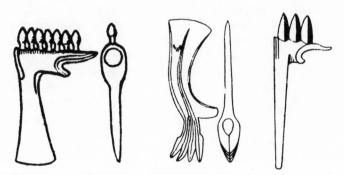

Fig. 85. **Socketed axe heads of bronze. The decoration over the socket represents either manes or fingers.**

"Sever the shoulder of Yam The Lord,
   Cut off the arms of Nahar, The River of Judgment."
But Yam was too strong,
   He did not fall.
Yam did not even waiver,
   He did not collapse.
So, Kothar-wa-Hasis forged another battle-ax,
   and christened it "Expeller!"
"Expel Yam,
   Expel him from his throne,
   . . . Nahar from his seat of power!   20
"Fly from the hand of Ba'al,
   Fly like an eagle from his fingers!
"Split the skull of Yam The Lord,
   Separate the eyes of Nahar, The River of Judgment!
"Now, Yam will fall,
   Collapse on the earth!"
   (Judg 5:27).

This second ax defeats Yam, but does not destroy him. Ba'al's victory gives him supremacy and he is proclaimed "King of The Gods."

Ba'al And Anat Battle Mot
(IV.vii)

A new House of Ba'al is constructed on the rain clouds. There is a remarkable window in the clouds through which Ba'al's thundering voice can be heard announcing the rain he sends to farms all over the earth (1 Kgs 18:36–45).

However, Mot, God of Death, sends the searing sirocco winds which dry up the moisture of Ba'al and all the plants die (Hos 13:14–15). Defiantly, Ba'al dispatches two messengers to Mot in The Underworld to defend his right to rule the earth.

Ba'al proclaimed,
. . . .
"I alone rule The Divine Assembly,
   Who, but I, can feed The Gods,   50
   Who, but I, can feed The People of The Earth?"
But Mot responded,
   The God of Death answered Ba'al's challenge:

(V.i)

"My appetite is like that of a lion,   *15*
   My energy like the dolphins in the sea.
Death is a pool luring the wild oxen (Ps 49:14),
   . . . a spring baiting herds of deer (Ps 42:1).
The dust of the grave devours its prey   *20*
(Eccl 3:20; Job 10:9),
   . . . eats whatever it wants with both hands (Prov 1:12).

. . . .

I will also devour the moisture of Ba'al (Ps 141:7),
   Suck the rain drops of The Son of El down my throat.
   . . . of El's Beloved, The Hero, into my mouth.   *35*

. . . .

Mot's lower lip stretches down to the earth,
   His upper lip reaches to the sky,
   He licks the stars with his tongue.
Ba'al's rain runs off into Mot's mouth,
   and down into his throat (Isa 5:14).

(V.ii)

The olives shrivel,   *5*
   The earth's produce dies,
   The fruit of the trees drops off (Hab 3:17).
Almighty Ba'al becomes frightened,
   The Rider of the Clouds is terrified.
"Go! Tell Mot, The Son of El,
   Deliver this message to El's Beloved, The Hero.   *10*
"Hear the word of Ba'al the Almighty,
   . . . the message of The Greatest Hero of All.
"I salute you, O Mot, Son of El,
   I will be your slave forever!" (Job 42:1–6).

Ba'al dies when the moisture from the rain withdraws deep into earth and the growing season comes to an end.

Ba'al's death is mourned by The Divine Assembly, especially El, his Father, and Anat, his wife. They perform the rituals of mourning typical in the ancient Near East, filling their hair with dust and slashing their bodies with knives (Jer 16:6; Ezek 27:30). Anat arranges a huge funeral and sacrifices hundreds of animals.

As a childless widow, Anat petitions Asherah, the wife of El, for a son to succeed Ba'al as King (Gen 38; Deut 25:5–10; Ruth 4). Asherah nominates two candidates.

First, Asherah said to El:

. . . .

"Make Yadi Yalhan king!"

. . . .

(VI.i)

But El the Kind said,
    El the Benevolent answered: *50*
"Yadi Yalhan is too feeble to take Ba'al's place,
    . . . to wield The Son of Dagan's spear."
Then, Asherah said,
    The Goddess of The Sea spoke:
"Make Athtar The Awesome king!"
    Let Athtar The Awesome become king!"
Then Athtar The Awesome climbed Mt. Zaphon,
    Ascended the throne of Ba'al the Almighty.
But his feet did not reach the footstool (Ps 132:7),   *60*
    His head did not touch the headrest.
Then, Athtar the Awesome spoke,

. . . .

"I cannot serve as king,
    I cannot dwell on the heights of Zaphon!"
So, Athtar The Awesome descended,
    Stepped down from the throne of Ba'al the Almighty.
He became king of The Underworld,
    Lord of The River of The Dead.

Anat now hunts down Mot to force The God of the Dead to release her husband. Using a legal gesture, she grabs the hem of Mot's tunic (1 Sam 24:4) and demands that Ba'al be raised from the dead. But Mot argues that Ba'al is no better than any other victim whom he harvests on his insatiable rounds of the earth.

Unable to get what she wants from Mot, Anat seizes him, chops him up with her sword, and sows the pieces like seeds in a field. Then she goes back to El and asks him to conjure a dream to deter-mine whether Ba'al is truly dead.

(VI.iii)

"If Ba'al the Almighty lives,
    If The Most High, The Lord of the Earth, breathes,   *5*
"Then in the dream of El the Kind, The Compassionate,
    In the vision of The Creator of All,

"—the heavens will rain oil (Ps 126:4),
—the dry stream beds will flow with honey (Jer 11:5).
"And I will know that Ba'al The Almighty lives,
    . . . that The Most High, The Lord of the Earth, breathes."

El has the vision and begins to laugh and celebrate when he realizes that Ba'al is alive and that the crops will bloom again. El tells Anat to talk with Shapshu, Goddess of The Sun, and ask her to look for Ba'al. Shapshu agrees, and begins by pouring wine into the dry furrows of the fields. There is a break in the text here.

    When the story resumes, Ba'al defeats both Yam and Mot to regain his title as King of The Gods.

(VI.v)

In the seventh year, Mot, The Son of El, spoke,
    Cried out to Ba'al the Almighty: *10*
"Because of you, Ba'al, I have lost face (Ps 132:18),
    Because of you, . . .
"I have been cut up with a sword,
    . . . burnt with fire.
"I have been ground with a mill stone,
    . . . winnowed with a sieve
    (Jer 15:7; 51:2).
"I have been scattered like seed in the fields,
    . . . sown in the sea! (Ps 129:3).
"Now give me something to eat,   *20*
    And let us make peace!"

(VI.vi)

Then, Mot ascended Mt. Zaphon,
    Went up to Ba'al, singing:
"Mot was strong, but Ba'al was stronger (1 Sam 18:7),
    They gored each other like wild oxen.
"Mot was strong, but Ba'al was stronger (Ps 124:1–5),
    They struck each other like serpents.
"Mot was strong, but Ba'al was stronger,   *20*
    They kicked each other like stallions.
"Mot was strong, but Ba'al was stronger.

. . . .
But Shapshu, Goddess of the Sun, shouted back,
    "Listen to me, Mot, Son of El!

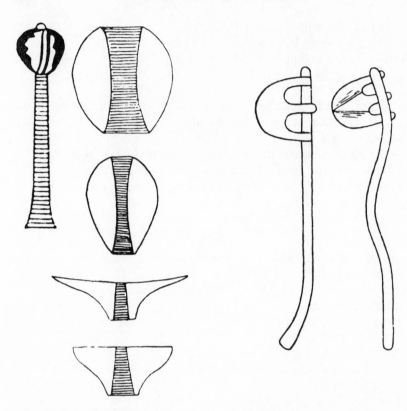

Fig. 86. **Mace heads in three shapes: apple, pear and saucer— as depicted on Egyptian monuments.**

Fig. 87. **Some typical war axes from Canaanite monuments and depictions.**

"You can never defeat Ba'al the Almighty,
    El, God of the Bull, your father, cannot ignore you.
"He will tear the door-posts out of your house (Judg 16:3),
    He will overthrow your throne,
. . . break your scepter in two!" (Ps 125:3).
Then, Mot, The Son of El, became frightened,   30
    The Beloved of El, The Hero, trembled at her words.
Finally, Mot capitulated,
    . . . .
"Let Ba'al be enthroned as king,
    Let his majesty endure forever!"   35

The Lament For Ur

"The Lament For Ur" *mourns the city of Ur destroyed by the Elamites and Subarians during the Ur III Period between 2200–2100 BCE. This version of the lament has been pieced together from over twenty separate clay tablets excavated at Nippur in southern Mesopotamia, which is today's Iraq. It was composed during the Old Babylonian Period between 2000–1500 BCE.*

Standard laments make broad use of repetition and refrain. "The Lament For Ur" contains four hundred and thirty-six lines which are divided into eleven songs. Each song is separated from the others by a colophon like "The First Song" and an antiphon like "Wind blows through the gate of his stall, wind moans pitifully through its doors, the cow has fled the barn." A similar technique appears in The Book of Psalms where doxologies like "Blessed be the Lord, the God of Israel, from all eternity and forever. Amen. Amen" (Ps 41:13) divide it into five sections.

Parallels to "A Lament For Ur" appear in The Books of Lamentations, Jeremiah, Ezekiel and in Psalm 22 and Psalm 137, which are laments for the city of Jerusalem destroyed by the Babylonians in 587 BCE.

The first song in "A Lament For Ur" is a litany naming Enlil, Ninlil, Inanna, Sin, Ningal, Enki and all the other gods who have abandoned Ur, Kesh, Isin, Uruk, Eridu, Ummah, Lagash and all the other cities in the urban alliance which were then destroyed. Each stanza follows the same form.

The ox has fled the barn,   *(1)*
  Wind blows through the gate of his stall.
The Lord of All the Lands has fled his temple,
  Wind blows through the gate of the city.

Fig. 88. **Votive tablets from Nippur showing scene of worship. Sumerian.**

Fig. 89. **Fragments of a bas-relief in the Louvre found at ancient Lagash showing typical Sumerian worshipers.**

Enlil has fled Nippur,
    Wind blows through the gate of the city, . . .
    Wind moans pitifully through its doors (Jer 15:7).   *(37)*

The second song is also a litany in which the members of The Divine Assembly order their sanctuaries to mourn the destruction of Ur. As in the first song, the form of each stanza is the same.

Put The Temple at Eridu in mourning,   *(62)*
    Until The Lord of Eridu can weep no more for Ur.

In the third song, Ningal laments the destruction of Ur in the ruins of The Temple of Nanna, her husband, who is God of the Moon and Guardian of Ur. She uses the term The Day of The Storm in the same way that the Hebrew Bible uses The Day of the Lord (Amos 5:18–20) or that day (Isa 24–27; Zech 12:1–9).

I mourned The Day of the Storm,   *(88)*
    The Day of the Storm fated for me.
My burden, the cause of my tears,
    The Day of the Storm fated for me.
My burden, predestined for me, a Goddess,   *(90)*
    The cause of my tears.

I trembled as The Day of the Storm drew near,
  The Day of The Storm fated for me,
My burden, the cause of my tears,
  The merciless Day of the Storm, fated for me.
I could not flee the cruel violence of that day,
  Its fury was greater than all the joys of my life.
I trembled as that night drew near,
  The Night of Tears fated for me.
I could not flee the cruel violence of that night,
  The storm's fury filled me with fear.
  The storm's destruction kept me from sleep.
That night, I could not go to bed (Job 7:13–14),
  That night, I could not fall asleep.   *(100)*
Night after night, I could not go to bed,
  Night after night, I could not fall asleep.
The Land of Ur is filled with sorrow,
  Sorrow fated for my land.
Should I scream for the life of my calf,
  Cry out for its release?
  I cannot save my land from its misery.
My land is in distress,
  Distress fated for my land.
Even if I could flap my wings like a bird,
  Even if I could fly to save my city,
Still my city will be destroyed,
  Still my city will be razed to its foundations,
  Still my Ur will be destroyed where it lays.

  In the fourth song, Ningal, like the widow of Tekoa (2 Sam 14:1–20), goes to The Divine Assembly and petitions Anu and Enlil to reverse their verdict to destroy Ur. They refuse.

"Spare my city from destruction!"
  I pleaded.
"Spare Ur from destruction!"
  I pleaded.
"Spare its people from death!"
  I pleaded with them.
Anu would not listen to me,   *(160)*
  Enlil would not countermand his order,
  . . . would not decree: "Grant this woman's petition!"

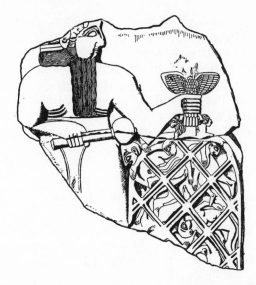

Fig. 90. **Sumerian picture of a warrior god Ningursu who holds his conquered enemies in a net. Note the symbol of the god as an eagle as the closure of the net. From the Stele of the Vultures in the Louvre.**

Instead, they ordered the city destroyed,
    They ordered Ur destroyed.
Its fate was sealed,
    Its people sentenced.

The fifth song describes The Storm which Enlil unleashes to destroy Ur. The song uses metaphors like drought, earthquake, tidal wave and fire storms to describe the invasion of Ur by its enemies.

Enlil prepares The Storm.
    The people mourn.
The winds bringing rain to the land, he withholds,
    The people mourn.
The good winds he stores in Sumer.
    The people mourn.
He gives the burning winds their orders.
    The people mourn.
He puts Kingaluda in charge,
    He makes him Keeper of The Storm.

He prepares The Storm of Death.
   The people mourn.
He prepares the burning winds.
   The people mourn.
Enlil and Gibil prepare The Sirocco.   *(180)*
   The people mourn.
The Sirocco howls.
   The people mourn.
The Storm of Death sweeps the earth.
   The people mourn.
The burning wind rushes unrestrained to the sea,
   Great waves swallow the city's ships.
Earthquakes rock the pillars of the earth,
   The people mourn.
Fire storms ignite and explode in the wind.
   The people mourn.
Fires flank the path of the wind,
   Searing as the desert heat,
   Scorching as the noon sun.
Dust shrouds the sun,
   Cuts off its life giving light.   *(190)*

    *The sixth song describes the aftermath of The Storm. Bodies
are piled high in the gate and the walls and buildings of the city are
in ruins.*

When The Storm subsided,
   The city lay in ruins.   *(210)*
The Temple of Nanna lay in ruins.
   The people mourn.
When The Storm subsided,
   The people mourn.
Bodies lay like broken pots,
   Scattered everywhere.
The walls were breached (Amos 4:3),
   The people mourn.
The main gates were blocked with corpses,
   The main streets were choked with dead.
Bodies filled the streets,
   Where crowds once celebrated festivals (Lam 4:5).
Bodies lay in every street,
   Corpses piled on every road.

In the squares, where people danced (Jer 9:21-22),
  Heaps of corpses lay.
Their blood filled every crevice,
  Like molten metal in a worker's mold.
Their flesh, like butter left in the sun,
  Melted from their bodies (Jer 16:4).
Warriors wounded by an axe,
  Lay unbandaged.

Warriors wounded by a lance,
  Lay in the dust,
  ... gasped like gazelles pierced by hunters' spears.   *(220)*
The judges of Ur were slaughtered,
  The people mourn.
The wise of Ur were scattered,
  The people mourn.
Mothers abandoned their daughters (Lam 4:3-4),
  The people mourn.
Fathers disowned their sons.
  The people mourn.
Women and children were abandoned,
  Their property looted.

In the seventh song, Ningal laments the destruction of Ur by cataloging every person, place and thing destroyed. After she lists each entry, the congregation chants "Alas!" or "Gone!" or "Woe!"

Fig. 91. **A Sumerian cylinder seal showing mythical conflicts between rampant lions and human/beast heroes. The bottom left scene may represent the Epic of Gilgamesh.**

All the buildings outside the walls—destroyed,
    Alas! (Amos 5:16)   *(261)*
My city, my innocent lamb—slaughtered (Jer 11:19),
    Its shepherd—Gone!   *(265)*
The daughters of Ur—taken by foreigners,
    Woe! (Isa 5:8–23)   *(283)*

The eighth song catalogs the calamities which have befallen Ur and Ningal, who no longer enjoys the offerings which Ur made to her as its Goddess. After each calamity, the audience chants "With Ur gone, how can Ningal survive?" The song concludes with a series of petitions seeking the rebuilding of Ur (Jer 30:4–5; 31:38–40; Ezek 37).

May Anu, The God of Gods, decree:
    "It is enough!"
May Enlil, The Lord of All Lands,
    Grant Ningal a better fate!
May he rebuild Ur,
    Restore your majesty!
May he return your city to its former grandeur,
    And make you, once again, its Queen!

The conclusion of "The Lament For Ur" repeats the petitions to Nanna initiated in the fourth song. They ask that Ur be spared from The Storm or rebuilt after its destruction.

The Book of Proverbs

The Book of Proverbs

The Teachings of Ahiqar

Ahiqar was an advisor to Sennacherib, who was king of Assyria from 704–681 BCE. In 1906, German archaeologists recovered an edition of his memoirs and teachings on the island of Elephantine which is today part of the city of Aswan in southern Egypt. The editors wrote in Aramaic about 500 BCE on eleven palimpsest or recycled sheets of papyrus, which had to be erased before they could be reused.

"The Teachings of Ahiqar" are an attempt by this aging civil servant to clear himself of the charge of treason. Despite all he had done for his country during his long and distinguished career, he himself never had a natural child who could be his successor. So, Ahiqar adopted Nadin and trained him to take over his job in the Assyrian court. However, once Nadin got into office, he betrayed Assyria. Since Ahiqar was Nadin's patron, he was also sentenced to death by the king.

"The Teachings of Ahiqar" contains sayings and analogies like those found in The Book of Proverbs and some fables like those in Judges 9:8–15 in which plants and animals taunt each other.

(vi)

Spare the rod,
   Spoil the child (Prov 13:24; 19:18).   *81*
Lions ambush stags, shed their blood, eat their meat   *88*
   When humans meet, the same takes place.
There are two kinds of people which are good,   *92*
   and a third which pleases everyone under the sun—
   (Prov 6:16–19; Hos 6:2)
—someone who shares his wine (Eccl 9:7),
   —someone who follows good advice,
   —someone who can keep a secret!

179

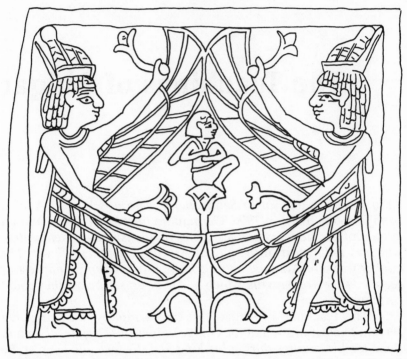

Fig. 92. **An ivory decoration piece from the Syrian city of Arslan Tash with winged godlike creatures protecting a figure.**

(vii)

Above all else, control your mouth,	*98*
Do not repeat what you have heard	
A human word is a bird,	
Once released, it can never be recaptured	
(Prov 26:2; Sir 27:16).	
Choose words carefully to teach another,	*99*
The word is mightier than the sword (Eccl 5:2).	
Rulers are often soft spoken,	
But their words are two-edged swords	*100*
(Ps 52:2; Heb 4:12).	
Never challenge the words of a ruler!	*101*
Should wood challenge the fire,	
Should flesh challenge the knife,	*104*
Should subjects challenge their rulers?	
(Isa 10:15; 45:9; Eccl 6:10).	

Gentle is the tongue of a king,   *105*
   But it can break a dragon's bones
   (Prov 25:15b; Sir 28:17).

(viii)

I have hauled sand,   *111*
   I have carried salt,
   But nothing is heavier than debt
   (Prov 27:3; Sir 22:14–15).
When the young speak mighty words   *114*
   They soar beyond them
   (Ps 8:2; Wis 10:21; Matt 21:16).
Their words may become oracles,
   and sometimes—with The Gods' help—even make sense!
Once there was a leopard,
   And a goat who was cold.   *118*
The leopard asked:
"Would you like my coat,
   Would you like me to cover you?"
The goat answered:
"What comfort is your coat?
   You only want my hide?"
A leopard does not approach a gazelle,
   Unless it is looking for blood.
In the eyes of God, a woodcutter working in the dark,   *125*
   . . . is a thief burglarizing a house
   (Eccl 10:9).

(ix)

Do not draw your bow or shoot your arrow at the innocent,
   God will come to their help,   *126*
   God will turn your own arrows back on you
   (Ps 11:2; 64:2–7; Jer 21:4–5).
Do not borrow from the wicked!   *130*
When you borrow money,
   Work night and day to repay it.
Receiving a loan is sweet. . . ,
   Repaying a loan may cost all you possess
   (Prov 6:1–5).
Do not be dissatisfied with your life.   *136*
   Do not covet the honors which Fate denies
   (Ps 131:1).

Those who do not honor their parents,   *137*
 Are cursed by The Gods for their evil
 (Prov 20:20; Exod 20:12; Deut 21:18–21).
Do not be greedy with your goods,   *138*
 Lest your heart become arrogant
 (Ps 62:10).

(x)

Do not compete with those more powerful than you, *142*
 Do not compete with those stronger than you,
 They will only add your power and strength to their own.
Staring at others' goods,
 Makes you unable to see your own.
Do not be sweet enough to swallow,   *148*
 Do not be bitter enough to be spit out!

(xi)

The thorn bush asked the pomegranate tree—   *165*
 "Why so many thorns to protect so little fruit?"
The pomegranate tree said to the thorn bush—
 "Why so many thorns to protect no fruit at all?"
 (Judg 9:8–15; 2 Kgs 14:9).

(xi)

If an unscrupulous creditor takes hold of your cloak, *171*
 Let him have it.
Divine Judge Shamash will take his garments,
 And give them all to you!
 (Exod 22:26–27; Deut 32:35).

(xiii)

Guard your master's well carefully,   *192*
 Next time he may entrust you with his gold!
A man to a wild ass—   *204*
"If you will let me ride you,
 I will let you live in my stable."
But the ass said to the man—
"You live in your stable,
 And I will not have to let you ride me!"
 (Job 39:5–8).

(xiv)

Do not send the Arab bedouin to sea,
  Nor the Phoenician sailor into the desert,
  Everyone's work is unique
  (Jer 13:23).

208

Fig. 93. **An Assyrian winged bull-man-god who served as protectors of gates and doorways. Called a cherubim in the Bible.**

The Teachings of Ptah-Hotep

Ptah-Hotep taught about 2450 BCE, during the Fifth Dynasty of the Old Kingdom in Egypt. Versions of Ptah-Hotep's teachings are preserved on papyrus sheets in hieratic or "longhand" Egyptian writing as well as on clay tablets in hieroglyphic Egyptian "printing." They were all recovered in Egypt around 1900 by archaeologists from France and are at the Bibliothèque Nationale in Paris.

In the ancient Near East, a teacher—like Ptah-Hotep—bore the title "Father" or "Mother" (Prov 1:8). A student was called "Child!" Teachers taught students to observe, to judge and to act. They used the saying (Prov 1:17) to hand on their observations; the masal or analogy (Prov 9:17; Prov 10:1) to hand on their judgments. Analogies linked together form an essay, which is the most common genre in "The Teachings of Ptah-Hotep." Introductory and concluding essays, which offer students general encouragement to excel in life, sandwich essays which provide advice on specific careers and professions into which they will graduate.

Students memorized the sayings and analogies of their teachers. Competent students, who could apply teachings and act accordingly, graduated—"Like golden apples in silver settings are words spoken at the proper time" (Prov 25:11). The incompetent, who could not apply what they learned, did not graduate—"A proverb in the mouth of a fool hangs limp, like crippled legs" (Prov 26:7).

"The Teachings of Ptah-Hotep" are widely echoed in The Books of Proverbs, Ecclesiastes and Sirach. Both traditions teach students how to avoid pride, get good advice (Prov 2:4), practice table manners (Prov 23:1; Sir 8:1; Sir 31:12), be reliable (Prov 25:13), make friends (Sir 6:7) and deal with women (Prov 6:24; Sir 9:1).

My students, in all things—
Be intelligent, not arrogant,
   Be wise, not over-confident.   *50*

184

Seek advice from the simple,
  As well as from the wise.
No one ever reaches their full potential,
  There is always more to learn.
Wisdom hides like emeralds,
  But it can always be uncovered—
—in a poor man,
  —in a young woman grinding grain
  (Prov 2:1–5; 19:20).
Now—
If you become *a ruler,*
  Do what is right,
  Stay above reproach.
Be just in your decisions,
  Never ignoring the law.   *90*
Injustice brings punishment,
  Injustice brings all your work to nothing.
Injustice brings success for a moment,
  Justice brings success for two generations . . .
  (Prov 11:21; 17:13).
If you *work for someone* else,   *120*
  Take what your master offers.
Do not look about with envy,
  Do not always hope for more.
Stand humbly until your master speaks to you,
  Speak only when spoken to.
Laugh when your master laughs,
  Try to please your master in everything.
But remember this—
  No one knows what is in another's heart
  (Prov 23:1–3).

Fig. 94. Egyptian scribes at work. Beni Hasan, 14th century B.C.E.

When masters are at the table,
　　They may seem to dispense favors as they see fit,
—to favor those who are useful,
—to favor those who think as they do.
But Ka, The Human Soul, is guided by The Gods,
　　Therefore do not complain about their choices.
If you become *a messenger* for the mighty,
　　Be completely reliable on every assignment.　　　　　*150*
Carry out your orders to the letter.
　　Withhold nothing,
　　Forget nothing,
　　Forge nothing,
　　Repeat nothing,
　　Embellish nothing.
Do not make harsh language worse,
　　Vulgarity turns the mighty into enemies
　　(Prov 25:13).
If you *work for the newly rich,*
　　Ignore their former lack of wealth and distinction.
Do not be prejudiced against them,
　　Do not detest them for once being lower class.
Respect them for their accomplishments,　　　　　*180*
　　Acknowledge them for their acquisition of property.
Property does not come of itself,
　　Property must be earned.
It is their law for those who wish it.
　　As for those who overstep, they are feared.
It is the gods who determine the quality of people.
　　God defends them even when they sleep. . . .
If you become *a judge,*
　　Listen patiently to the plaintiff's suit.
Give plaintiffs time to air their cases,
　　Plaintiffs want petitions heard more than granted.
If you interrupt plaintiffs,　　　　　*270*
　　If you are rude to petitioners,
　　People will complain: "Why does the judge do that?"
To grant every petition is unnecessary,
　　To hear every petition calms passions, prevents violence.
If you become *the owner of a house* or are a *house guest,*　　　　　*280*
　　Stay away from the women of the house!
Keep your mind on business, your eyes off pretty faces.

Foolish dreamers become casualties of unwise actions
    (Prov 6:23–26; 7:24–27).
Escape love sickness and lust,
    And succeed in everything else you do
    (Prov 6:27–29).
If you *inherit property,*
    Take only your own portion of the estate,
    Do not covet the portions of others.
Those who respect the property of others earn respect,   *320*
    Those who defraud others lose their own property.
To covet even a small thing,
    Is to convert the peaceful into warriors!
    (Prov 15:27).
If you become a *landowner,*
    Establish a household,
    Be faithful to your wife.

Fig. 95. An early portrayal of an
Egyptian scribe. 5th Dynasty
(about 2500 B.C.E.).

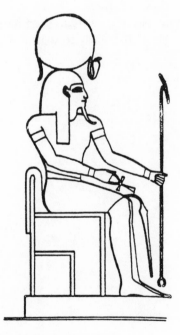

Fig. 96. Typical Egyptian portrayal
of the god Atum.

Feed her, clothe her, make her happy,   *330*
   And she will provide you with an heir.
Do not sue her in court,
   But do not let her dominate you.
To judge a woman's moods,
   Is to read a woman's eyes.
A wife who shares her husband's wealth,
   Is a wife who is faithful to her husband
   (Prov 12:4; 31:10–11 + 27–31).
If you are *promoted,*
   Be generous with the wealth The Gods give you,   *430*
   Take care of your home town now that you can
   (Eccl 6:2–3).
Finally, my students, remember—
The wise follow their teachers' advice,
   Consequently, their projects do not fail.
The wise rise to positions of trust,
   Guided by their teachers' instruction
   (Hos 14:10).
The wise rise early to start to work,
   Fools rise early to worry about all there is to do.

The Teachings of
Amen-em-ope

Amen-em-ope taught in Egypt between 1200–1000 BCE during the late New Kingdom period. Shortly after 1900, archaeologists recovered two versions of "The Teachings of Amen-em-ope." One version was written in hieratic Egyptian longhand on papyrus sheets and is now in the British Museum (#10474) in London. The other version is on a clay tablet and is in Turin, Italy.

"The Teachings of Ptah-Hotep" and "The Teachings of Amen-em-ope" demonstrate the consistency of Egypt's world view over the 2000 years separating one tradition from the other. For example, both contrast the wise and foolish. In "The Teachings of Amen-em-ope," the wise are soft-spoken or "silent," whereas the fool is hot-tempered or "hot-headed." The wise are soft-spoken because they know when to talk and when to listen. Fools, on the other hand, are hot-tempered because they let anger run or ruin their lives. The same imagery still appears in Christian wisdom literature like James 3:1–18 (100 CE).

However, there are striking differences between one tradition and the other. For example, "The Teachings of Ptah-Hotep" emphasize direct action and offer students a clear-cut strategy for success. "The Teachings of Amen-em-ope," on the other hand, place more importance on patience. Likewise, in "The Teachings of Ptah-Hotep," the wise strive for advancement while being generous with the fruits of their success, whereas, in "The Teachings of Amen-em-ope," the wise have few material comforts and little wealth. They are self-controlled, modest, thoughtful in speech, considerate of others and humble servants of The Gods. Despite these virtues, however, it is acknowledged that the wise are not perfect, since perfection is the possession of The Gods alone.

189

Despite the fact that there may have been many Hebrew slaves in Egypt prior to 1250 BCE, there were strong cultural ties between Israel and Egypt during the period of the Israelite monarchy after 1000 BCE. For example, The Book of Proverbs 22:17—24:22 closely parallels "The Teachings of Amen-em-ope." Both follow the same format—a general introduction followed by thirty chapters of surprisingly similar advice on specific topics—"Have I not written for you thirty sayings of admonition and knowledge, to show you what is right and true, that you may give a true answer to those who sent you?" (Prov 22:20–21).

The Words of The Wise
Chapter One
(iii)

Listen to what I say,
    Learn my words by heart.   *10*
Prosperity comes to those who keep my words in their hearts,
    Poverty comes to those who discard them!
Enshrine my words in your souls,
    Lock them away in your hearts
    (Prov 22:17–18).
When the words of fools blow like a storm,
    The Words of The Wise will hold like an anchor.
Live your lives with my words in your heart,
    And you will live your lives with success.

(iv)

My words are a handbook for life on earth,   *1*
    My words will bring your body to life.

Fig. 97. **Scribes recording the bringing of gifts. Beni Hasan.**

Chapter Two

Do not steal from the poor,
   Nor cheat the cripple
   (Prov 22:22).
Do not abuse the elderly,
   Nor refuse to let the aged speak,
Do not conspire to defraud anyone, yourself,
   Nor encourage anyone else's fraud.
Do not sue those who wrong you,   *10*
   Nor testify against them in court.
Injustice can turn on fools quicker than—
   ... floods eroding the bank of a canal,
   ... north winds bearing down on a boat,
   ... storms forming,
   ... thunderbolts cracking,
   ... crocodiles striking.
Fools cry out,
   They shout to The Gods for help.

(v)

Let Thoth, God of the Moon, judge their crimes,   *1*
   But you steer the boat to rescue them.
Do not treat fools,
   The way fools treat you.
Pull the fool up out of high water,
   Give the fool your hand.
Leave the punishment of the fool to The Gods,
   Feed them until they are full,
   Give them your bread until they are ashamed
   (Prov 25:21–22).

Chapter Three

To stop and think before you speak—
   ... is a quality pleasing to The Gods.

Chapter Four
(vi)

The fool who talks publicly in the temple,
   ... is like a tree planted indoors.   *1*
A tree indoors blooms,
   But then withers,
   ... it is thrown into the ditch,

... it floats far from home,
... it is burned as trash
(Jer 11:16, 17:5–8; Ps 1; Ezek 17:5).
The wise who are reserved,
  are like a tree planted in a garden.
A garden tree flourishes,
    Doubles its yield,
    ... its fruit is sweet   *10*
    ... its shade is pleasant,
    ... it will flourish in the garden forever.

Chapter Six
(vii)

Do not relocate the surveyor's stone to steal a field,
  Nor move the surveyor's line to take a farm
  (Hos 5:19).
Do not covet another's land,
  Nor poach on the widow's field   *15*
  (Prov 22:28, 23:10).
To forge a claim to the public path through a field,
  Cries out to Thoth, God of the Moon, for justice.
Those who seize public lands,
  Are the enemies of the weak—
The enemies of public life,
  Are the destroyers of whatever they see.
Those who steal from the community,
  Are those whose warehouses are robbed,
  Are those whose heirs are defrauded of their inheritance.

(viii)

Do not topple markers on the boundaries of a field,   *10*
  Lest your conscience destroy you.
To please The Pharaoh, Our Lord and God,
  Observe the borders of your neighbors' fields
  (Prov 23:11).
To please The Pharaoh, The Lord of All,
  Maintain the borders of your own field.
Do not plow across the boundary furrow of your neighbors,
  And your neighbors will not plow across yours.
Plow only your own fields,
  Eat only bread from your own threshing-floor—
  —there will always be enough.

Fig. 98. **Workers slaughtering cattle for food. Beni Hasan.**

Better a single bushel from God,
  Than five thousand stolen bushels   *20*
  (Prov 15:16, 16:8).

(ix)

Stolen grain does not make good bread in the bowl,   *1*
  Nor good feed in the barn,
  Nor good beer in the jar.
Stolen grain only spends the night in your granary,
  At dawn it vanishes.
Better is poverty from the hand of God,
  Than wealth from a granary full of stolen grain
  (Prov 19:1, 22).
Better is a single loaf and a happy heart,
  Than all the riches in the world and sorrow
  (Prov 15:17, 17:1).

Chapter Seven

Do not spend tomorrow's riches,
  Today's wealth is all you own   *10*
  (Ps 39:6, 49:5, 52:7, 62:10; Eccl 5:10).
Do not set your heart on material goods,
  Time makes beggars of us all.
Do not work to lay up a surplus,
  Toil only for what you need
  (Prov 23:4; Eccl 3:12).
Stolen goods only spend the night,
  At dawn they vanish.
Dawn reveals where stolen goods spent the night,
  But they have vanished
  (Ps 62:10; Prov 21:6; 23:5).
At night, the earth opens its mouth,   *20*
  And renders its verdict on stolen goods.

(x)

At night, the earth consumes stolen goods,   *1*
　　And absorbs them into the underworld.
At night, stolen goods dig a hole into the underworld,
　　They fly away like geese into the sky
　　(Prov 23:5).

Chapter Nine
(xi)

Do not take counsel with fools,
　　Nor seek their advice
　　(Prov 22:24).
Do not speak back to superiors,
　　Nor insult them.
Do not let superiors discuss their troubles with you,
　　Nor give them free advice
　　(Prov 6:2).
Seek advice from your peers,
　　Do not ignore your equals.   *20*

(xii)

More dangerous are the words of fools,   *1*
　　Than storm winds on open waters. . . .

(xiii)

Do not rush to embrace fools,   *8*
　　Lest their advice drown you like a storm
　　(Prov 22:25).

Chapter Eleven

Do not covet the goods of the poor,
　　Nor hunger for their bread.
The goods of the poor will stick in your throat,
　　You cannot swallow them.

(xiv)

Those who perjure themselves to defraud the poor,
　　Lie only to steal from themselves (Prov 23:6–7).   *10*
Success obtained by fraud cannot last,
　　The bad only spoils the good.

When you vomit a piece of bread too large to swallow,
  What you gained is lost . . . (Prov 23:8).

Chapter Thirteen
(xv)

Do not cheat your neighbor with false ledgers,
  And horrify The Gods.
Do not bear false witness,
  And destroy your neighbor with your words
  (Prov 14:5).
Do not over-assess the property of your neighbor,
  And inflate what you are owed.
If a poor neighbor owes you a great debt,
  Forgive two-thirds, collect one
  (Prov 22:26–7; Matt 18:27).

20

Fig. 99. **Egyptian nobleman fishing in the papyrus marshes of the Nile. Beni Hasan (19th century B.C.E.).**

(xvi)

Make honesty your guide to life,
    And you will sleep soundly, and wake happily.   *10*
Better to be praised for loving your neighbor,
    Than loving your wealth.
Better is bread eaten with a contented heart,
    Than wealth spent with sorrow . . . (Prov 17:1).

Chapter Eighteen
(xix)

Do not go to bed worrying,   *11*
    Wondering: "What will tomorrow bring?"
    (Prov 27:1; Ps 31:15).
No one knows what tomorrow brings,
    The Gods are perfect, but humans fail.
Human words are one thing,
    Divine actions are another
    (Prov 16:9, 19:21).
Do not say, "I am innocent!"
    And then file a lawsuit!
    (Prov 20:9).
Judgment belongs to The Gods,
    Verdicts are sealed by divine decree.   *20*
Before The Gods, no one is perfect,
    Before The Gods, everyone has failings.

(xx)

Those who always strive for perfection,   *1*
    Can destroy it in a moment.
Control your temper,
    Save your life.
Do not steer your life with your tongue alone!
Make your tongue the rudder of your boat,
    But make Amon-Ra its pilot.

Chapter Twenty

Do not bear false witness against your neighbor,
    Nor defame the righteous.

(xxi)

Do not court the favor of those in white,   1
   And ignore those in rags!
Do not take bribes from the powerful,
   And oppress the poor for their sake.
Justice is the gift of The Gods,
   Given to whomever they will. . . .
Do not alter the decrees which The Gods have written,
   Nor do damage to the designs of The Gods.
Do not claim the power of The Gods,   15
   For you are subject to Fate and Fortune.

Chapter Twenty-Five
(xxiv)

Do not make fun of the blind,
   Nor tease the dwarf,
   Nor trip the lame   10
   (Prov 17:5).
Do not tease the insane,
   Nor lose patience with them when they are wrong
   (1 Sam 21:14).
Humans are clay and straw,
   The Gods are their sculptors
   (Ps 103:14; Isa 29:16; 45:9; 64:9).
Every day The Gods tear down,
   And every day they build up.
The Gods can make a time for thousands to be powerful,
   . . . and a time for thousands to be powerless
   (Prov 29:13; Eccl 3:1–10).
Blessed are those who journey to The Land of the Dead,
   They will be safe in the hands of The Gods.   20

Chapter Twenty-Eight
(xxvi)

Do not arrest the widow gleaning your fields,
   Nor fail to be patient with her reply   10
   (Ruth 2:2–9).
Give the stranger olive oil from your jar,
   And double the income of your household
   (1 Kgs 17:12–16).
The Gods desire respect for the poor,
   More than honor for the powerful.

Fig. 100. **Egyptians in boats on the Nile recover the body of a drowned man (Beni Hasan, 19th century B.C.E.).**

Chapter Thirty

To study these thirty chapters,
    Is to be educated and entertained!
    (Prov 22:20).
These are The Book of Books,
    They give the wisdom to the simple.
Blessed are those who teach them to the simple,
    They are pleasing to The Gods
    (Hos 14:9).
Fill your soul with these teachings,
    Put them in your heart
    (Deut 6:4–8).
Master these teachings,
    Hand them on to others.
The skilled Scribe,
    Will become Pharaoh's Servant
    (Prov 22:29).

The Books of Job
and Ecclesiastes

The Story of Keret

"The Story of Keret" *appears on three clay tablets written in the cuneiform script using Ugaritic, an alphabetic language. This version of the story was composed about 1400 BCE by Ilimilku The Scribe.*

The story describes the trials of a king whose children all die. Overcome with the weariness of his task, Keret falls asleep and dreams. In his dream, The God El tells him to go to war and capture a bride and begin a new family with her. Keret obeys and becomes so successful that he revolts against his divine patrons, who punish him for his pride (hubris) by destroying his health. Nonetheless, El once again intervenes and Keret recovers only to have his own son, Yassib, revolt against him!

There are major and minor parallels between "The Story of Keret" and the Hebrew Bible. In many ways, Keret's family tragedies and personal sickness are like those of Job. Keret's dreams are like those of Jacob (Gen 28:10–17) and Solomon (1 Kgs 3:4–15). The revolt of his son Yassib parallels the revolt of David's son, Absalom (2 Sam 15:1–6), against him. The pride or hubris motif is most familiar to western audiences from the Greek epic literature.

(I.i)

The House of King Keret, once home to seven, to eight,
   —all sons of a single mother—was ruined.
Keret's soul was despondent (Job 1:13–19),   *10*
   His palace vacant.
His wife had died,
   His companion was gone.
Three sons died at birth,
   A fourth son of disease,
   A fifth son of fever,

A sixth was lost at sea,
A seventh died in battle.   *20*

. . . .

Keret locked himself in his room and wept,
    Going over each tragedy again and again. . . .
Exhausted from weeping, he fell asleep,
    Soaked with tears he began to dream. . . .   *30*
El appeared to him in his dream (Gen 28:10–22),
    The Father of the Gods came to him in a vision.
El appeared and asked Keret:
"Keret, why are you crying?
    Why is The Son of El in tears?   *40*
Act like your father—El, God of the Bull,
    Be strong like The Father of All."

. . . .

"Give me sons!" Keret pleaded
    "I need a family!" he begged.
El replied:
"Stop your weeping, Keret,
    Dry your tears, Son of El.
Wash your face with water,
    Rub your skin with oil.

(I.ii)

Bathe your arms to the elbow,   *10*
    Scrub the dirt from your fingertips to your shoulders.
To your tents!
    Prepare for war!
Pick out the sheep with your right hand,
    . . . a lamb in each hand.
Assemble all the food needed for a sacrifice.
    . . . a bird suitable for sacrifice,
Pour wine from a silver cup,
    . . . honey from a golden bowl.
Climb to the top of the tower,   *20*
    Climb to the heights of the wall.
Raise your hands to heaven,
    Sacrifice to your father, El, God of the Bull."

*After El has taught Keret how to offer the sacrifice, he tells him
to gather a six-month supply of food for an army of 300,000 warriors
who will lay siege to Udum. The army was not to attack the walls of*

the city, but cut them off for seven days (Josh 6) until King Pabil sues for peace. El told Keret to seal the treaty by marrying Pabil's daughter, Hurriya.

(II.iii)

"Give me what The House of Keret lacks,   *38*
  Give me the Lady Hurriya, . . .
She will bear the children of Keret,   *48*
  . . . sons for The Son of El."

Keret follows the instructions of El, and the text repeats almost exactly the sequence of events described in the dream. However, one deviation does occur. On the third day of his journey, Keret stops at the shrine of the goddess Asherah and makes a vow (Judg 11:30–31; 1 Sam 14:24):

(II.iv)

"By the power of Asherah, Goddess of Tyre,
  By the power of The Goddess of Sidon,
If I can marry Hurriya,   *40*
  If I can bring this woman into my court,
Then I will give you double her bride price in silver,
  . . . three times her value in gold."

Fig. 101. **Portrayal of a Phoenician city in an Assyrian wall relief showing a lower rampart, a high mound and inner walled city on the top.**

The second tablet then chronicles the celebration of the royal marriage which is also celebrated by The Assembly of The Gods.

(II.v)

When The Divine Assembly had convened,
   The Mighty Ba'al proposed a toast.
"May El the Kind, the Compassionate, bless Keret the Noble,
   . . . Show favor to The Son of El."
El took his cup in his hand,
   his goblet in his right hand,
El blessed his servant, Keret the Noble,   *20*
   . . . showed favor to The Son of El.
"Keret, you have obtained a wife (Job 42:10–15),
   You have taken a woman into your house,
   . . . a maiden into your court.
She will bear you seven sons,
   Eight sons she will bear you,
   . . . and daughters.
Even to the youngest,
   I will give the first-born's possessions."

. . . .

As time passed, Hurriya does give birth to many sons and daughters. But Keret does not fulfill his vow to Asherah. As a result, she inflicts him with a fever no one could cure. Keret's ministers and family went into mourning to prepare for the death of the king. Finally, El hears their prayers and responds by polling the other gods to see if any of them could cure Keret. None of the gods can do it, so El empowers The Goddess Shataqat to cure him (2 Kgs 4:34–37; 5:10–14).

(III.vi)

"Death—be vanquished!" El orders,   *1*
   Shataqat—be strong!" he commands.
Shataqat sets out from The Divine Assembly,
   And comes to The House of Keret.
She enters to the sounds of crying,
   Sobbing filled the palace.
She wipes the sweat from his brow,
   She lets his appetite return,   *10*
   . . . his taste for food come back.
Death was vanquished!
   Shataqat was victorious!

Then Keret the Noble commanded,
  He shouted in a mighty voice:
"Hear me, Lady Hurriya,
  Butcher a lamb for me to eat,
  ... mutton for my dinner."

Keret once again sits upon his throne and all appears to be well.
However, Keret's illness gives his son Yassib a chance to seize the
throne (2 Sam 15:1-6), so he challenges Keret to abdicate.

"Listen to me carefully!" Yassib threatens:
"If enemies had invaded the land while you were ill,
  They would have driven you out,
  Forced you into the hills (2 Sam 15:14).
Your illness made you derelict:
  You did not hear the case of the widow (Prov 29:14-16),
You did not hear the case of the poor (Amos 2:6-7),
  You did not sentence the oppressor (Amos 5:12),
You did not feed the orphan in the city,
  ... nor the widow in the country   *50*
  (Isa 10:2; Ezek 22:7).
The sickbed has become your brother,
  the pallet your closest friend.
Step down from the kingship,
  Allow me to reign.
Relinquish your power,
  Let me sit on the throne."

The text breaks off as Keret calls on the gods to take revenge on
this rebellious son.

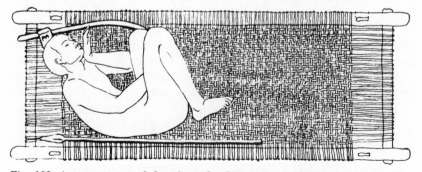

Fig. 102. **A reconstructed drawing of a Syrian burial in which the warrior**
has a spear behind him and the axe before him.

The Sufferer and The Soul

"The Sufferer and The Soul" *is a dispute over suicide composed during the time of the Middle Kingdom in ancient Egypt between 2050–1800 BCE. It was written on papyrus sheets, the tops of which were already destroyed when archaeologists recovered them shortly before 1900. They are now preserved in the Berlin Museum as Papyrus Berlin 3024.*

During the First Intermediate Period between 2258–2050 BCE, the social, political and economic structures of Egypt came apart. Consequently, teachers began to reevaluate Egypt's world view as well. "The Sufferer and The Soul" *files a lawsuit against Egypt for its views on Life and Death. At the trial, The Sufferer is the attorney for Death and Ka, The Soul, is the attorney for Life. Teachers in Mesopotamia and in ancient Israel use similar trial genres in such works as The Books of Ecclesiastes and Job.*

"The Sufferer and The Soul" *evaluates various responses to the phenomenon of* Weltschmerz *in people who conform to all of society's expectations, but who get sick of living when their efforts get them nowhere. This literature does not present solutions to suffering, it simply studies it.*

In "The Sufferer and The Soul," *The Sufferer proposes committing suicide as an antidote to pain and failure. The Soul, on the other hand, argues that suicides are not eligible for the appropriate funeral services, which disqualifies the dead from the pleasures of the afterlife, and their survivors of any public support! Then, The Soul argues that funerals are a waste of time for rich and poor alike. As an alternative to suicide, The Soul proposes that The Sufferer just stop conforming to society's expectations and start enjoying life. The Soul closes its counter-argument with two parables to which The Sufferer responds with four laments. The first lament equates The Soul's advice with a series of putrid metaphors; the second lists*

*all the reasons why death is preferable to life when things are bad;
the third describes death as a friend who will free suffering human
beings from their painful lives, and the fourth promises that all
those who die will live happily ever after with The Gods. The first
lines in each stanza of each lament are the same.*

Hear me out, my Soul—   *1*
My life now is more than I can bear,
   Even you, my own Soul, cannot understand me.
My life now is more terrible than anyone can imagine.
   I am alone.
So, come with me, my Soul, to the grave!
   Be my companion in death. . . .
If you cannot take away the misery of living,
   Do not withhold the mercy of dying from me.
Open The Door of Death for me!   *20*
   Is that too much to ask?
Life is only a transition,
   Even the trees fall.
Crush out this evil life,
   Put an end to my misery
   (Job 3:17–19).
Let Thoth, The Divine Judge, hear my case,
   Let Khonsu, The Pharaoh's Guardian, protect me.
Let Ra, The Divine Boatman, judge me,
   Let Isis . . . defend me.
Listen, my human Friend—
It is so foolish for an ordinary human like you,
   To want the funeral of a king!

Fig. 103. **Portrayal of a funeral procession on ships across the Nile. The
mourners and internal organs ride in the first boat, the body of the deceased in the second. Beni Hasan.**

But, my Soul—
I cannot die without arranging a proper funeral,
  Only when Death is a thief are funerals unprovided.
But, if you help me,
  I can rest in peace in The Land of the Dead.   *40*
Then, I will take you with me to the grave,
  I will care for your tomb like your child.
I will shade you from the heat of the sun,
  I will make wandering souls envious of you. . . .
However, if you continue to oppose my death,   *50*
  You will never find rest in The Land of the Dead.
Trust me, my Soul, my companion,
  My heir will carry out my last wishes.
My heir will stand beside my tomb on the day of burial,
  My heir will carry my body to its grave.
Now listen, my human Friend—
There is no such thing as a happy funeral,
  Funerals always make people cry.
You just carry the body out of the house,
  And bury it on a sterile and sunless hillside.   *60*
Even granite chapels and pyramids decay,
  Monuments forgotten as soon as the builders are gone,
—pitiful as paupers' graves on the banks of The Nile,
  —buried without funerals,
—with only The Nile as a pallbearer,
  —the Sun as an embalmer,
  —the Fish as mourners.
So, listen to me,
  Take my advice!
Enjoy living!
  Stop worrying!
You have heard the parable about death—
Once, a man plowed a field,
  Loaded the harvest on a barge,   *70*
  And towed the barge to market.
At sunset, a terrible storm came up,
  The man, in town, survived,
But his wife and children, at home, perished,
  Lost when their houseboat capsized in Crocodile Lake.
The man sat down and mourned:
"Should I weep for a wife, buried without a funeral,
  And thus, who cannot be raised to a new life?

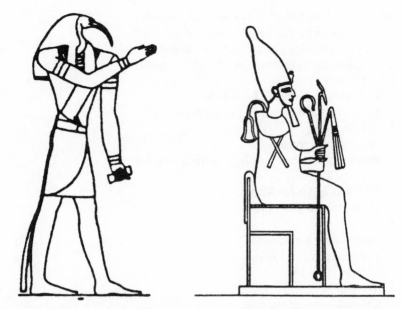

Fig. 104. **The Egyptian god Thoth.**   *Fig. 105.* **The Egyptian god Osiris.**

"Or should I weep for a child,
   Buried before it had even one life to live?"   *80*
And you also know the parable about the stubborn man—
Once a man ordered his wife to serve all her food at noon,
   But she refused—
   "This food is for our supper!"
The man stormed out of the house,
   Arguing with himself as he went back to work.
When the man came home,
   He was still furious.
Why wouldn't he listen to his wife's advice,
   Why couldn't anyone in his family reason with him?
My Soul, do you really want me to go on living—
When my life smells worse than—
   . . . bird drop on a hot day,
   . . . rotten fish in the full sun,   *90*
   . . . the floor of a duck coop,
   . . . the sweat of fishermen,
   . . . a stagnant fish pond,
   . . . the breath of a crocodile?

When my reputation is worse than someone—
    ... accusing a faithful woman of adultery,
    ... calling a legitimate child a bastard,   100
    ... plotting to overthrow the government?
Can't you see?
    Everyone is a thief (Jer 9:4-5),
    There is no love among neighbors.
Can't you see?
    Hearts are covetous,
    People take what belongs to their neighbors.
Can't you see?
    The just have perished,
    Fools are everywhere.
Can't you see?
    Everyone chooses evil,
    Everyone rejects good
    (Amos 5:14-15).
Can't you see?   110
    Crimes outrage no one,
    Sins make everyone laugh.
Death stands before me today,
    Like Health to The Sick,
    Like Freedom to The Prisoner.
Death stands before me today,
    Like the smell of myrrh,
    Like a canopy on a windy day.
Death stands before me today,
    Like the perfume of the lotus,
    Like sitting in The Land of Drunkenness.
Death stands before me today,
    Like a well-beaten path,
    Like a soldier returning home from war.
Death stands before me today,
    Like clear skies after a rain,
    Like a treasure hidden in a field.   140
Death stands before me today,
    Like Home to The Traveler,
    Like his Native Land to The Exile.
Surely, whoever goes to The Land of the Dead,
    Will live with The Gods,
    Will judge the sins of the wicked.

Surely, whoever goes to The Land of the Dead,
　　Will ride in The Barque of the Sun,
　　Will collect gifts offered at temples.
Surely, whoever goes to The Land of the Dead,
　　Will be wise,
　　Will have a hearing before Ra The Creator.

My human Friend—
Throw your cares on the fire with your offerings,   *150*
　　Get on with your life.
Stay with me here,
　　Stop thinking about dying.
When it is time for you to die,
　　When your body returns to the earth,
Then, I will travel with you,
　　And we shall live together forever!

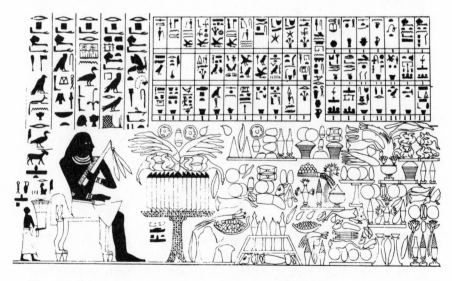

Fig. 106. Scene from the tomb of a nobleman where the deceased is seated
before rich foods to feed him in the afterlife. Beni Hasan.

The Farmer and The Courts

"The Farmer and The Courts" *is part of the Berlin papyrus (#3023, 3025) recovered by archaeologists before 1900. It contains the protests of an eloquent peasant who argues for his rights in the courts of Egypt during the First Intermediate Period (2258–2052 BCE). Narrative sections of prose introduce nine exchanges, which are composed in poetry, between the farmer and various judges. The teachers who composed* "The Farmer and The Courts" *during the Middle Kingdom Period (2134–1786 BCE) clearly felt that the events took place in a time of unrest caused by political and social instability in Egypt.*

Parallels to "The Farmer and The Courts" *appear in more than one literary movement in ancient Israel. The Books of Judges and Ruth also reflect the prejudice of a later period that earlier times were lawless. The Prophets in ancient Israel champion human rights for the poor in much the same language as the farmer's. The Book of Job follows a structure similar to* "The Farmer and The Courts." *In both, the petitioner is forced to make one plea after another, seemingly without hope of relief, until suddenly it is granted and his goods are restored. Finally, both The Wisdom of Solomon and* "The Farmer and The Courts" *stress that while individual human beings may die, the justice they do (Wis 8:13) and their good names last forever (Wis 1:15).*

(R)

Once, there was a farmer named Khun-Anup, who lived in The Salt-Field District near Thebes. One day he said to Marye, his wife: "I am going down to the city for food. Go into the barn and see how much grain is left from last year's harvest." After determining that there were twenty-six measures of barley, the farmer took six with him to trade and left the rest to feed his family.

The farmer loaded the asses with salt, reeds, leopard skins, wolf   *10*
hides, doves and other goods from his district to trade. Then he set
out for the city. He traveled south toward Herakleopolis through
Per-fefi, north of Medenit. Tut-nakht, son of Isri—who was an offi-   *40*
cial of The Chief Steward, Rensi, the son of Meru—was standing on
the bank of the canal and saw the farmer coming.

As he watched the farmer approach, Tut-nakht said to himself:
"I think I have a scheme I can use to steal this farmer's goods!" (1
Kgs 21:1–4).

At one point the public path along the embankment of the
canal in front of Tut-nakht's house was no wider than a loincloth.
One side of the path was flooded with water, and the other side was
overgrown with barley from Tut-nakht's field. Tut-nakht told one of
his slaves: "Get me some clothes from my house!" When the slave
brought them, Tut-nakht laid the clothes down over the water.   *50*

(B1)

Just then, the farmer came down the path. Tut-nakht shouted
to him: "Be careful, you farmer! You are about to step on my
garments."

The farmer answered: "I am being careful! I do not wish to
offend you, but your garments are right in my way. I cannot climb
the steep embankment along the canal on one side of them, nor do I
want to trample the grain in your field on the other. Please give me
permission to pass."

As he stood there talking, one of the asses bit off a stalk of   *10*
barley. Then Tut-nakht said: "Now I am going to confiscate your ass

Fig. 107. **Scene from a tomb at Beni Hasan showing workers in a vineyard picking and crushing grapes, fishermen, and a cattle tender bathing the herd.**

for eating my grain. I will sentence it to the threshing floor for this offence."

But the farmer pleaded: "My intentions are good. Only one stalk has been damaged. If you do not let me pay for the damage done and buy back my donkey, I will appeal to Rensi, the son of Meru, who is The Chief Steward and Governor of this district. Is it likely that he will allow me to be robbed in his own district?"

Tut-nakht answered, "Why do the poor always want to speak to   *20* masters? You are speaking to me, not to The Chief Steward!" Then he took a stick and beat the farmer and confiscated his asses.

The farmer protested his painful sentence and the injustice done to him.

Tut-nakht tried to silence him in the name of Osiris, The God of Silence.

The farmer protested the attempt to silence him and swore by   *30* Osiris that he would not keep quiet until his property was returned.

For ten days, the farmer appealed to Tut-nakht without results. So, he went to Herakleopolis to appeal to Rensi, the son of Meru, who was The Chief Steward. As he was rushing off to board his barge, the official asked the farmer to file his protest with a lower court, which finally took his statement.   *40*

Eventually, Rensi and his council considered the case and decided that Tut-nakht was guilty only of harassing a farmer who no longer worked for him and should be sentenced only to return the farmer's goods. However, Rensi did not announce the verdict. So the farmer went to see about his appeal in person.   *50*

"You are The Chief Steward,
    You are my lord!
"You are my last hope,
    You are my only judge.
"When you sail The Lake of Justice,
    Fairness fills your sail!   *60*
"You father the orphan,
    You husband the widow.
"You brother the divorced,
    You mother the motherless
    (Deut 10:18).
"I will extol your name throughout the land,
    I will proclaim you a just judge!

"... a ruler without greed (Ps 22:22–6),
  ... a great man without fault.
"... a destroyer of lies,
  ... a just judge, who hears the cry of the poor
  (2 Sam 15:4).
"Hear me when I speak,
  Give me justice.
"Relieve me of this burden of poverty,   *70*
  ... the care which weighs me down!" (Ps 25:17).

The farmer appealed to Rensi in the name of Neb-kau-Ra, Pharaoh of Upper and Lower Egypt.

So, Rensi went to The Pharaoh and said: "My lord, I am hearing the case of a truly eloquent farmer. His goods have been stolen by a man in my service and he has come to me for justice."

The Pharaoh said: "I am ordering you to keep this man waiting without giving him any reply. Just keep him talking. You must write   *80* down each of his speeches and send them to me. Furthermore, without letting this farmer know, I want you to provide for his wife and children as well as for his own needs."

Each day, a friend of The Chief Steward delivered ten loaves of bread and two jars of beer to the farmer. Rensi also ordered the governor of The Field-of-Salt District to deliver three measures of grain to the farmer's wife every day.

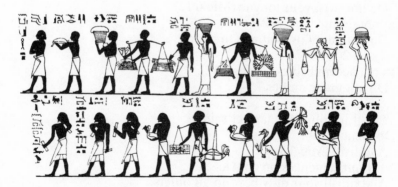

Fig. 108. **Servants carrying abundant food and goods to the tomb of the deceased for the afterlife. Beni Hasan.**

The second time the farmer comes to see about his appeal, The Chief Steward asks him whether these goods were really worth going to prison over.

The farmer replies.

"The Distributer puts more grain in his own pile,   *105*
    The Giver of Full Measure shorts his people.
The Lawmaker approves of robbery,
    —who is left to punish the wrongdoer?—
The Inspector condones corruption.
One is publicly criminal,
    The other tolerates injustice
    (Amos 5:10–13).
Do not learn from such as these!
Punishment lasts for a moment,
    Injustice goes on forever.
Good example is remembered forever,
    Follow this teaching—   *110*
'Do unto others,
    As you would have others do unto you'
    (Matt 7:12).
Thank others for their work,
    Parry blows before they strike,
    Give jobs to the most qualified.
. . . .
Make your shoreline a shelter,   *130*
    Clear out the crocodiles which infest your landing.
Speak the truth (Hos 10:4),
    Do not twist your tongue (Mic 6:12),
Do not perjure yourself,
    Do not bear false witness in court
    (Exod 20:16).
Do not accept bribes (Amos 5:12),
    Do not graze on lies."
. . . .
The third time, the farmer said:
"Do justice,
    And live! (Mic 6:8).
Carry out sentences on convicts,
    And fulfill your duty beyond all others.
Does the hand-scale lie? (Mic 6:11)
    Is the stand-scale tilted? (Amos 8:4–6).   *150*
    Is Thoth, God of The Scales, looking the other way?

Do not be tempted by corruption . . .
>   Do not return evil for good (Amos 5:14),
>   Do not substitute lesser for better goods.

. . . .

Do not steal,
>   Do not make deals with thieves,   165
>   Greed is blind (Job 20:20).

Close your eyes to violence,
>   And no one will punish criminals.

Ferry only those who can pay,
>   And you become an honest man gone bad,
>   . . . a shopkeeper who gives no credit to the poor."

When the farmer made this appeal before The Chief Steward   185
at the gate of the court, Rensi had two guards arrest him and flog
him.

Nonetheless, the farmer said:
"The Son of Meru continues to do evil.
>   He sees, but does not see,
>   He hears, but does not hear (Isa 6:10),
>   He ignores what he is told" (Job 24:12).

. . . .

The farmer eventually makes nine appeals to Rensi. In each
appeal, the farmer recites all the wrongs done to him, describes
Egypt as a topsy-turvy world where lawgivers become lawbreakers,
and appeals to Rensi and others in authority to take their respon-
sibilities seriously and give him justice. In one final burst of frustra-
tion, the farmer decides that his only hope for justice will be in the
afterlife where Anubis is The Divine Judge (Job 10:20–22; 14:7–14).

(B2)

"Since you will not grant my appeal,   115
>   I will take it before Anubis himself."

Then, Rensi, the son of Meru and The Chief Steward, sent two
guards to arrest the farmer. The farmer was frightened, thinking he
was about to be sentenced to death.

Fig. 109. **Scenes from daily work in Egypt. Beni Hasan, 19th century B.C.E.**

"Death long-desired arrives like water for the thirsty,
   ... like the first drop of milk on a baby's tongue"   *120*
   (Job 5:26; 7:1–10).

    *But Rensi reassures the farmer that no harm will come to him.
Then he orders the transcripts of the farmer's appeals, which he had
sent to Pharaoh Neb-kau-Ra, to be read aloud and The Pharaoh's
judgment to be announced. Tut-nakht is summoned to the court*   *130*
*and given an inventory of all the property which he is ordered to
return to the farmer.*

The Sufferer and The Friend

"The Sufferer and The Friend" *is a theodicy, a dialogue about human misery composed in Babylon about 1000 BCE using cuneiform script. Since 1900 archaeologists have recovered only enough clay tablets to reconstruct twenty-seven stanzas with eleven lines each. In this acrostic poem, the first letters in each couplet spell out "I am Saggil-kinam-ubbib, Priest, Cantor, Servant of The Gods and The King."*

The form of "The Sufferer and The Friend" *is similar to The Book of Job. Both are conversations, dialogues or arguments. The theme of* "The Sufferer and The Friend" *is similar to The Book of Ecclesiastes. Both argue that a world filled with suffering and evil proves The Gods cannot be just! For example, he was born to aging parents who soon died and left him an orphan, but The Gods did not protect him.*

The Sufferer
Come, O wise one, let me speak to you. . . .   *1*
Where can one find a sage of your abilities?   *5*
   Where is there a scholar of your wisdom?
   Where is the counselor who will hear my grief?
I am without resources,
   . . . lost in the depths of despair.
When I was a child. . . ,
Fate took my father from me,
   The mother who bore me went to The Land of No Return.   *10*
   My parents left me an orphan.

Fig. 110. **A terra-
cotta figurine of
Phoenician type.
Found at Ayia Irini.**

The Friend
Your tale is sad my friend.
    But you have thought too long of evil things.
You have blinded yourself to common sense.
    You have scarred your face with frowns.
Parents die,
    They cross The River.
If anyone could choose . . .
    Who would not choose to be rich?
Those who serve The Gods will be protected,
    Those who fear The Goddesses will prosper
    (Mic 6:8).

The Sufferer
Your thoughts soothe like The North Wind,
    . . . bring relief.

20

My friend, you give good advice,
    But let me say one word about it.
Those who ignore The Gods prosper.   *70*
    Those who pray constantly are homeless and destitute
    (Jer 12:1; Job 21:7–16).
As a young man. . . ,
I sought the will of The Gods,
    I prayed to The Goddesses and fasted.
But prayer and fasting got me nowhere.
    The Gods decreed poverty, not wealth, for me.
The cripple and the fool outrun me,
    The criminal is promoted, I am fired.

The Friend
The criminal will lose the position you so desire,   *235*
    His . . . is soon gone.
The criminal will take wealth amassed without The Gods,
    His riches will become the prey of thieves
    (Job 18:5–21).
If you do not seek the will of The Gods,
    What hope is there for success?
Those who submit to the yoke of The Gods never hunger,
    . . . eat when food is scarce.   *240*

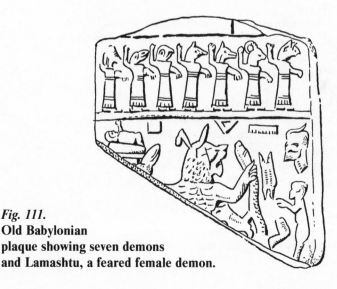

Fig. 111.
**Old Babylonian
plaque showing seven demons
and Lamashtu, a feared female demon.**

Seek the soothing wind of The Gods,
>   And a year's losses will be restored in a moment
>   (Job 8:5–7).

The Sufferer
I have searched the world for order,
>   But all is turned upside down
>   (Eccl 3:16).

. . . .
>   The Gods do not even stay the course of a demon.
The father tows his boat through the canal,
>   While his son lies idly in bed.
The elder son struts about like a lion,
>   While the younger son must be content as a teamster
>   (Gen 25:27).
The elder son walks the street without concern,
>   While the younger son gives food to the poor.   *250*
What good has it done me to bow down to The Gods?
>   When now I bow before the dregs of society,
>   —who, as if they are rich, treat me with contempt.

The Friend
You are wise and knowledgeable,
>   But you have hardened your heart,
>   You accuse The Gods falsely
>   (Job 15:2–4).
The mind of The Gods is as unfathomable as the heavens,
>   The way of The Gods is beyond human understanding
>   (Job 11:7).
Among all the creations of Aruru,
>   The eldest is. . . .
A cow's first calf may be a runt,
>   While the second is big and healthy.   *260*
The first child may be born a weakling,
>   While the second is a valiant warrior.
Though one may witness the will of The Gods,
>   No one can understand it.

The Sufferer
Listen, my friend, to my words,
>   . . . to my well-chosen argument
>   (Job 21:2–3).

People praise the powerful who kill.
  But persecute the powerless, who are innocent.
People listen to the wicked, who despise The Gods,
  And ignore the honest, who obey them   270
  (Amos 5:10).
People fill the storehouse of the wicked with gold,
  And steal the beggar's bowl.
People lend a helping hand to the powerful. . . ,
  But trample the needy under foot
  (Amos 2:7).
Poor as I am, I am still oppressed,
  Despite my insignificance, I am persecuted by a nobody!

The Friend
When Enlil, Ruler of The Gods, created humans,
  When Ea The Glorious pinched them from the clay. . . ,
When Mami, Mother and Queen, shaped them,
  The Gods gave humans twisted speech.
The Gods empowered them to speak lies,
  . . . to speak falsely for all time to come   280
  (Job 15:5).
So . . .
People flatter the rich like kings,
  Talk to them like gods.
People treat the poor like thieves,
  Slander them like criminals.
People plot to kill the poor,
  Impose fines on them because they are powerless.
People terrorize the poor to death,
  Snuff out their lives like a flame.

The Sufferer
You have been kind, my friend,
  Now behold my affliction,
Help me in my distress,
  Understand my suffering.
I am a humble servant of The Gods,
  Yet, there is no one to help me.   290
I walk quietly through the city square,
  I whisper, I do not cry out.
I keep my eyes down,
  I look only at the earth.

I do not join other citizens at worship,
  I do not even stand with slaves.
May The Gods who abandoned me,
  Now have mercy on me!
May The Goddesses who abandoned me,
  Now have mercy on me!
May Shamash The Good Shepherd,
  Once again shepherd his people as he should!

Fig. 112. **A grain-goddess, seated, presents grain to a male vegetation god, perhaps Tammuz. Sumerian.**

The Song of Songs

Egyptian Love Songs

Many of the analogies in The Book of Proverbs are nearly identical with the teachings of Egyptian sages. Likewise, even though these "Egyptian Love Songs" are nearly one thousand years older than those in The Song of Solomon, the parallels are unmistakable. Egyptian cultural, political and economic influence in Canaan was at its peak during the 18th–20th dynasties (1570–1197 BCE). Egyptian-trained officials administered Canaan. They were schooled in Egypt's culture as well as its bureaucracy. The Egyptian military and foreign service stationed personnel in Canaan's administrative centers. Governors in Palestine appointed by Pharaoh sent their children to school in Egypt. Admiration and imitation of all that was Egyptian was inevitable, even by Egypt's colonies and slaves!

This copy of The Papyrus Harris 500 was recovered at Thebes from the Ramesseum complex in the Karnak Temple. The following excerpts are taken from an anthology from 1314 BCE, consisting of seventeen love songs divided into three separate groups.

Her song: *1*
   . . . I am still here with you,
But you are no longer here with me.
   Why have you stopped holding me?
Has my deed come back upon me?
   . . . the amusement.
If you seek to caress my thighs. . . ,

. . . .
Would you leave me to get something to eat?
   Are you that much a slave to your belly?
Would you leave me to look for something to wear?
   And leave me holding the sheet?

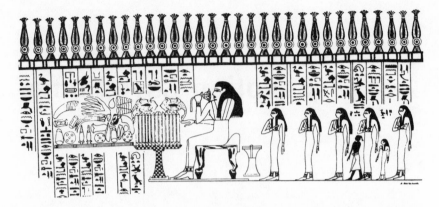

Fig. 113. **A deceased Egyptian woman enjoying a rich banquet in the after-life attended by her children and servants. Beni Hasan.**

If you are thinking about something to eat,
  Then feast on my breasts, make my milk flow for you.
Better a day in the embrace of my lover . . .
  Than thousands of days elsewhere. . . .

Her song: 2
Mix your body with mine,
  Like . . .
  Like honey mixes with water,
  Like mandrake mixes with gum,
  Like dough mixes with . . .
Come to your lover,
  Like a horse charging onto the field of battle,
  Like a falcon swooping toward the marsh . . .

. . . .

His song: 3
My lover is a marsh lush with growth. . . ,
Her mouth is a lotus bud,
  Her breasts are mandrake blossoms (Cant 7:13–14),
Her arms are vines,
  Her eyes are shaded like berries,
Her head is a trap built from branches . . .
  . . . and I am the goose!
Her hair is the bait in the trap . . .
  . . . to ensnare me (Cant 7:5).

Her song:
My cup is still not full from making love with you,
  —my little wolf, you intoxicate me (Cant 4:10).
I will not stop drinking your love (Cant 5:1),
  Even if they batter me with sticks into the marsh,
Even if they beat me into Syria,
  Even if they flog me with palm branches into Nubia,
Even if they scourge me with switches into the hills,
  Even if they whip me with rushes into the plains
I will not take their advice,
  I will not abandon the one I desire!

His song: 5
I am sailing north with the current,
  Pulling the oar to the captain's command.
My bed is ready for a lover,
  I am headed for a holiday at Memphis.
I will pray to Ptah, the Lord of Truth,
  That a lover will sleep with me tonight!
The Nile makes me drunk with love (Cant 2:10–13),
  I see Ptah in the reeds.
Sekhmet in the lotus leaves,
  Yadit in the lotus buds.
Nefertem in the lotus blossoms.
. . . .
Just thinking of a woman lightens my load,
Memphis is a jar of sweet mandrake (Cant 7:13),
  Set before Ptah the Gracious.

His song: 6
I will lie down inside my house,
  I will pretend to be sick (2 Sam 13:4–6; Cant 5:8).

Fig. 114. **Egyptians fishing in a canal or the Nile. Beni Hasan.**

Then my neighbors will come in to see,
    And my lover will come with them.
She will put the doctors to shame,
    She knows how to cure my illness (Cant 2:5).

His song: 7
My lover is the lady of a great house,
    Whose entrance is right in the middle!
Both doors are left wide open,
    The bolt is unfastened (Cant 5:2–6).
And my lover is furious!
If she hired me as her doorman,
    At least when I made her angry,
I would get to hear her voice,
    Even as I tremble like a child.

Her song: 8
I am sailing north,
    On the Canal of Pharaoh.
I turn into the Canal of Pre,
    I will pitch my tent overlooking the canal.
I have raced without rest,
    Since I first thought of the Canal of Pre.
I can already see my lover. . . ,
    He is heading for the Houses of. . . .

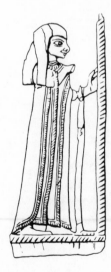

Fig. 115. **A noble woman from a painting from the
Canaanite city of Megiddo**

I will stand with you at the entrance to the Ity canal,
   You will lead me to Heliopolis.
As we walk away,
   . . . into the trees of the Houses of . . .
I gather branches,
   And weave them into a fan.
We will see if it works,
   And sends me on my way to the Garden of Love.
My breasts are smothered with fruit,
   My hair glistens with balm (Esth 2:12; Ruth 3:3).
When I am with you . . .
I am a noble woman filled with pleasure,
   I am the Queen of Egypt!

The Book of Daniel

The Visions of Neferti

"The Visions of Neferti" begins with Pharaoh Snefru (2680–2565 BCE) summoning Neferti to entertain him. Neferti announces the downfall of the Old Kingdom and the establishment of a new dynasty by Amen-em-het I (1991–1786 BCE), during whose reign "The Visions of Neferti" was composed. They extol the accomplishments of Amen-em-het, and try to persuade him to extend his control eastward to prevent further invasions of Egypt from Syria-Palestine.

There is one complete version of "The Visions of Neferti" on papyrus in the Leningrad museum (1116B). It was made during the 18th dynasty (1570–1305 BCE). However, numerous other fragments of the text have also been recovered since 1900.

Both "The Visions of Neferti" and The Books of Kings (1 Kgs 13) and Daniel (Dan 2–6) use the motif of entertaining a king with the prediction of his downfall. The motif of the slave who would be king in "The Visions of Neferti" also appears in The Story of Hagar (Gen 16; 21).

". . . your majesty, there is a Lector-Priest in Bastet named   *10*
Neferti. He is a valiant citizen, an accomplished scribe and a wealthy man."

Pharaoh Snefru ordered: "Bring him to me!"

Neferti prostrated before The Pharaoh.

Then, Pharaoh Snefru ordered: "Speak Neferti! Entertain me with well-chosen words and artful phrases!" (Dan 4:6).

Neferti asked: "Majesty, do you wish to hear what-has-hap-
pened or what-is-to-come?"   *15*

Pharaoh answered: "Speak to me of what-is-to-come. Today is passed!" and he summoned a scribe to write down everything Neferti told him.

235

Fig. 116. **The "Narmer Palette" showing the first king of a united Egypt victorious over his rivals from the Delta region. The two sides are a combination of pictures and hieroglyphics giving the king's name and titles. About 3000 B.C.E.**

Stir yourself, my heart,   *21*
   Cry for this land where you were born.
Do not commit evil by failing to speak.
   Those who could speak have been expelled,
   The powerful have been cast aside.
Do not be too weary to clarify the facts,
   Rise to the task before you!
Behold!
Officials no longer administer the land,
   What should be done is left undone.
May Ra ordain a day of restoration (Dan 9:16–19),
   For the land is in chaos,
No order remains,
   No profit can me made.
No one cares about the pain in this land,

No one sheds a tear for Egypt,
No one cries out: "What will be its fate?"
(Ezek 9:4).
The sun is shrouded,
  The Sun never shines,   *25*
  The people cannot see,
There is no life,
  The sun is covered in clouds,
  Everyone is dulled without it.
I can tell you what I see before me,
  I do not tell what will not be:
The canals are dry,
  They can be crossed on foot.
One searches for enough water to sail,
  The canals have turned into dry land.
Dry land replaces water,
  The canals have turned into dry land.
The south wind defeats the north wind,
  There is now just a single wind.
A strange bird will nest in the marsh,
  ... make its nest near the people,   *30*
The land is weak,
  Egypt cannot survive.
All good things perish,
  Fish-eating birds devour ponds of fish.
All good things perish,
  Egypt bows under the weight of invaders from Asia.
Enemies arise in The East,
  Asia ravages Egypt.
Fortresses lack soldiers and supplies. . . ,
No guard hears or sees the enemy of the night,
  —who scales the walls with ladders,
  —who slips through the fortress gates,
  —who ambushes the garrison in its sleep,
... I alone stand watch through the night.   *35*

Fig. 117. **Egyptian scene of bird hunting with traps. Beni Hasan.**

Desert herds will drink from the Nile,
    ... settle on these shores without fear.
The land is unsettled,
    Egypt is without direction.
As the saying goes ...
    "The mute leads the blind and the deaf."
I can describe it for you ...
The land is in torment,
    What is happening should never happen.
Take up arms (Dan 11:14),
    The land is in turmoil.   *40*
Soldiers stockpile arrows,
—to eat blood, not bread,
—to laugh at the wounded.
No one weeps for the dying,
    No one mourns and fasts,
    Everyone looks after their own welfare
    (Judg 21:25).
No one mourns for another,
    Every heart goes astray.
Everyone turns their backs on murder,
    ... while one kills another.
Your own son is your enemy,
    Your own brother is your foe,
    Sons slay their own fathers!   *45*
Everyone says: "I want,"
    All hope is lost.
Egypt is full of corruption!
Laws are enacted, but ignored.
    What was enacted is never obeyed.

Fig. 118. **Beni Hasan tomb painting (19th century B.C.E.) showing dark Egyptians battling lighter-skinned Asiatics.**

The property of a citizen is seized,
   ... and given to strangers.
I can show you ...
Landowners are in need,
   Strangers are prosperous.
Those who do not work are paid,
   Workers are not.
Debts are only paid under threat,
   Sentences are imposed only at spear point.
Lips profess: "You shall not kill!"
   Hearts burn with anger to destroy.   *50*
Egypt's land is scarce,
   Its rulers are many.
   (Dan 11:2-4)
Egypt is poor,
   Its officials grow rich.
Egypt's harvest is small,
   Its taxes are great.
The Sun withdraws from The Earth,
   The Sun shines, but there is no day.
No one knows the time,
   No one can see his shadow.
The face of The Sun does not dazzle the sight,
   No eyes fill with water.
The light of The Sun is like the light of The Moon,
   ... the shape remains unchanged,
   ... the light still touches the face of The Earth.
I can show you a land in distress ...
The weak exercise power (Dan 11:20-24),
   The master bows to the slave.
I can show you a society turned upside down ...
The hunted tracks the hunter,
   The Living search for Death.
Beggars are rich,
   The rich steal to survive.
The poor have bread,
   Slaves are set free.
The district of Heliopolis has vanished,
   The birthplace of The Gods is no more.
But a new Pharaoh will come from the South (1 Kgs 13:2),
   Amen-em-het the Triumphant will be his name.
The slave's son will wear the white crown,

The son of Nubia will wear the red crown.
He will unite The Two Lands of Egypt,　　　　　　　　60
　　He will have a firm grip on the oar,
　　He will put a steady hand on the tiller.
Happy are those who will live in his time (Dan 12:1),
　　Their names will last forever.
He will execute the conspirator,
　　He will silence the traitor.
He will conquer Asia,
　　He will burn Libya.
He will exile the revolutionary,
　　He will imprison the spy.　　　　　　　　65
The Winged Serpent will guard his brow,
　　Uraeus will protect him from rebels.
He will rebuild the fortresses,
　　He will drive the invaders from Asia away.
They will humbly ask for water,
　　. . . to allow their herds to drink.
Order will be restored to its rightful place,
　　Chaos will be forced to flee.
Happy are those who serve this Pharaoh!
The wise will pour out an offering for me,
　　When they see that what I have said has happened.

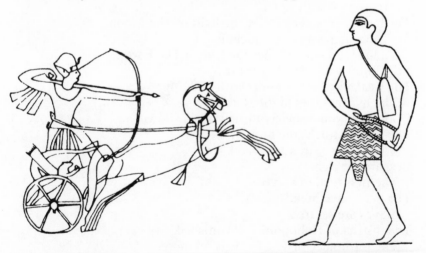

Fig. 119. **Pharaoh Rameses II in his war chariot at the battle of Kadesh in Syria.**

Fig. 120. **An Egyptian soldier trained as a rock slinger. Beni Hasan.**

Appendix

Outline of Mesopotamian History

2900–2400   Sumerian Period—city states: Kish, Uruk, Ur, Lagash. Gilgamesh, cuneiform, ziggurat

2400–2100   Akkadian Period—Sargon I (c. 2371–2316), Naram-Sin (c. 2291–2255); Ebla rivals Akkad

2200–2113   Ur III Period—Sumerian Revival, Ur-Nammu (law code), Shulgi

2006–1792   Amorite Period—struggle between Assyrians and new dynasties founded by Amorite leaders (Amurru) based at Larsa, Mari, and Babylon.

1792–1750   Reign of Hammurabi, unified most of Mesopotamia and compiled law code

1595–1168   Kassites ruled southern Mesopotamia for 400 little-known years. Aided by the overthrow of Hammurabi's dynasty during the brief invasion of the Hittites.

Hittites—centered in Asia Minor, they had two periods of prominence: Old Hittite Kingdom (c. 1600–1500) and the New Hittite Kingdom (c. 1375–1200). Suppiluliumas, Hattusilis

Hurrians—kingdom of Mitanni dominated western Syria from c. 1500–1370; Nuzi. Their defeat by the Hittites created a political vacuum filled by the Hittites and Assyrians (Tigris River area). Ugarit—seacoast city in Northern Syria, a trading center and nominal go-between for the Hittites and Egyptians between 1600–1200. Its alphabetic cuneiform literary texts closely parallel Old Testament poetic style: Aqhat, Baal and Anath. This period of history was brought to an abrupt end with the invasion of the Sea Peoples (including the Philistines) who, c. 1200, conquered the Hittites, destroyed Ugarit, and nearly conquered Egypt.

883–612	Neo-Assyrian Period—conquer Mesopotamia and Syro-Palestine in savage campaigns. Tiglath-pileser III, Shalmaneser III, Sargon II, Sennacherib, Ashurbanipal
612–539	Neo-Babylonian (Chaldean) Period. Nebuchadnezzar, Nabonidus, Belshazzar
539–331	Persian Period. Cyrus, Darius, Xerxes, Artaxerxes
331	Alexander the Great conquers Persians and Hellenistic Period begins; Seleucids, Ptolemies

Fig. 121. **Sumerian Cylinder seal showing the combat of Marduk against the winged dragon Zu.**

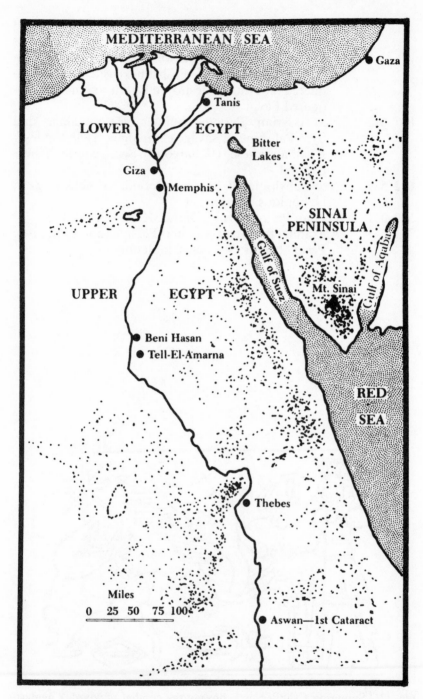

Fig. 122. **The land of Ancient Egypt. Giza marks the boundary between Lower Egypt in the Delta area, and Upper Egypt extending southward along the Nile.**

Outline of Egyptian History from 3100–332 BCE

3100–2700 Early Dynastic Period—Dynasties 1–2; Memphite royal culture, home provincial centers

2700–2200 Old Kingdom—Dynasties 3–6;
Third Dynasty (2700–2650): Zoser and the step pyramid at Sakkarah;
Fourth Dynasty (2650–2500): Pyramid Age, Giza pyramids of Cheops, Chephren, Mycerinus;
Fifth, Sixth Dynasties (2500–2200): Pyramid Texts

2200–2050 First Intermediate Period—Dynasties 7–10

2050–1800 Middle Kingdom—11th and 12th Dynasties

1730–1570 Second Intermediate Period—Dynasties 13–17

1570 Hyksos expelled from their capital, Avaris/Tanis, in the Delta region by Ahmose I, founder of the 18th dynasty

1570–1165 New Kingdom—Dynasties 18–20: Empire period (1465–1165);
Eighteenth Dynasty (1570–1305): Thutmose III (1490–1436), Akenaton (1369–1353), Tutankhamen (1352–1344), Haremhab (1342–1303)
Nineteenth Dynasty (1303–1200): Ramses II (1290–1224), Merneptah (1224–1200)
Twentieth Dynasty (1200–1090): Ramses III (1195–1164), attack of the Sea Peoples

1150–663 Post-Empire Period—Dynasties 21–26; decline of power and culture, several non-Egyptian Pharaohs: Sheshonk (945–924), Necho II (610–595)—Battle of Carchemish in 605; Story of Wen-Amon

525   Persian Conquest by Cambyses
332   Conquest by Alexander the Great and beginning of
             Hellenistic Period: founds Alexandria. Ptolemaic
             rulers until absorption by Rome in 30 BCE

Outline of Israelite History

A. Premonarchic periods portrayed in the Biblical text:
1. Ancestral Period—Abraham/Sarah, Isaac/Rebekah, Jacob/Rachel and Leah (date uncertain)
2. Movement of Jacob/Israel's family into Goshen, Egypt, Joseph (perhaps dated to Hyksos Period, c. 1750–1570)
3. Exodus from Egypt—Moses and Aaron (perhaps in the reign of Rameses II, c. 1290–1226)
4. Settlement Period—Joshua, Merneptah Stele, incursions of the Sea Peoples, Philistines (c. 1250–1150)
5. Judges Period—Ehud, Deborah, Gideon, Jephthah, Samson (c. 1200–1020)

B. Monarchy Period
1. Early Monarchy—Samuel and Saul (c. 1020–1000)
2. United Kingdom—David and Solomon (c. 1000–922)
3. Divided Monarchy—Israel survives until 721 and Judah until 587

Names to remember in Israel: Jeroboam (1st king), Ahab and Jezebel; Prophets—Elijah, Elisha, Amos, Hosea. Capital city—Samaria; Conquered by Assyrian king Sargon II in 721—population deported. Samaritans created by intermarriage of Jew and non-Jew.

Names to remember in Judah: Rehoboam (1st king), Jehoshaphat, Hezekiah, Josiah; Prophets—Isaiah, Micah, Jeremiah. Capital city—Jerusalem; Conquered by Nebuchadnezzar of Babylon in 597—Jehoiachin, Ezekiel and others taken into exile; final fall of Jerusalem in 587/6 with 2nd deportation to Babylon.

Fig. 123. Asiatics shown on a tomb wall at Beni Hasan (19th century B.C.E. They are dressed in "coats of many colors" typical of Canaan, and bring with them musical instruments, bellows for ironworking, and gazelles for sale.

Fig. 124. A scene of Asiatics at Beni Hasan.

C. Exilic and Post-Exilic Period

1. Babylonian Exile (597–538): Ezekiel, Isaiah of Exile
2. Persian Period (538–336): Cyrus, Darius, Xerxes, Artaxerxes; Temple rebuilt (515), Zerubbabel, Haggai; Jerusalem's walls rebuilt (c. 445), Nehemiah; Renewal of covenant by Ezra (c. 400).

D. Hellenistic and Roman Period

1. Conquests of Alexander of Macedonia (336–323) ended Persian control over Judah. All of Palestine became a part of the Hellenistic empire, ruled first by the Ptolemies and after 198 by the Seleucids. Maccabean revolt vs. Seleucid king Antiochus IV (Epiphanes) in 168 brought brief independence period (Hasmoneans).
2. Roman general Pompey captures Jerusalem in 63 BCE. Two unsuccessful revolts against Roman rule in 66–73 CE (when Herod's temple is destroyed) and the Bar-Kochba revolt in 132–135 CE. Jews were scattered throughout the Roman empire in the Diaspora.

Bibliography of Texts in Transcription and Transliteration

The Enuma Elish Story:

L.W. King, *The Seven Tablets of Creation* (2 vols., 1902).

A. Deimel, *Enuma Elis* (2nd ed., 1936).

S. Langdon, *The Babylonian Epic of Creation* (1923).

R. Labat, *Le poème babylonian de la création* (1935).

A. Heidel, *The Babylonian Genesis* (1942).

W.G. Lambert and S.B. Parker, *Enuma Elis: The Babylonian Epic of Creation* (1966).

The Atrahasis Story:

W.G. Lambert and A.R. Millard, *Atra-Hasis: The Babylonian Story of the Flood* (1969).

W.G. Lambert, "A New Look at the Babylonian Background of Genesis," *Journal of Theological Studies* 16 (1965): 287–300.

A.R. Millard, "A New Babylonian Genesis Story," *Tyndale Bulletin* 18 (1967):3–18.

The Story of Ra and The Serpent:

E.A.W. Budge, *Egyptian Hieratic Papyri in the British Museum*. First Series (1910).

R.O. Faulkner, *The Papyrus Bremner-Rhind* (1933).

The Memphis Creation Story:

K. Sethe, *Das "Denkmal memphitishcher Theologie," der Schabakostein des Britischen Museum* (1928).

J. Junker, *Die Gotterlehre von Memphis* (1940), no. 23.

M. Lichtheim, *Ancient Egyptian Literature. A Book of Readings,* vol. 1 (1975), 51–57.

The Story of Gilgamesh:
Peter Jensen, *Assyrisch-babylonische Mythen und Epen* (1900).
R. Campbell Thompson, *The Epic of Gilgamesh* (1930).
A. Heidel, *The Gilgamesh Epic and Old Testament Parallels* (1946).
J.H. Tigay, *The Evolution of the Gilgamesh Epic* (1982).

The Story of Anubis and Bata:
Select Papyri in the Hieratic Character from the Collections of the British Museum, II (1860), Pls. ix–xix.
G. Moller, *Hieratische Lesestucke,* II (1927), 1–20.
A.H. Gardiner, *Late-Egyptian Stories* (1932), 9–29.
M. Lichtheim, *Ancient Egyptian Literature. A Book of Readings,* vol. 2 (1976), 203–211.

The Treaty of Ramses II and Hattusilis III:
E.F. Weidner, *Politische Dokumente aus Kleinasien* (1923), 112–123.

The Story of Sargon's Birth:
L.W. King, *Chronicles Concerning Early Babylonian Kings,* II (1907), 87–96.

The Story of Balaam:
J. Hoftijzer and G. Van Der Kooij, *Aramaic Texts from Deir 'Alla* (1976).
J.A. Hackett, *The Balaam Text from Deir 'Alla* (1980).

The Code of Hammurabi:
E. Bergmann, *Codex Hammurabi: textus primigenius* (1953).
G.R. Driver and J.C. Miles, *The Babylonian Laws* (2 vols., 1952).

The Sumerian Code:
A.T. Clay, *Yale Oriental Series, Babylonian Texts,* Vol. I, no. 28.
J.J. Finkelstein, "Sex Offenses in Sumerian Laws," *JAOS* 86 (1966), 355–72.
———, "The Laws of Ur-Nammu," *JCS* 22 (1968-69), 66–82.

The Hittite Code:
J. Friedrich, *Die Hethitschen Gesetze* (1959).
E. Neufeld, *The Hittite Laws* (1951).

The Middle Assyrian Code:

G.R. Driver and J.C. Miles, *The Assyrian Laws, Edited with Translation and Commentary* (1935).

R. Yaron, "Middle Assyrian Laws and the Bible," *Biblica* 51 (1970), 77–85.

The El Amarna Letters:

C. Bezold and E.A.W. Budge, *The Tell El-Amarna Tablets in the British Museum* (1892).

J.A. Knudtzon, *Die El-Amarna-Tafeln* (1907–1915).

W.L. Moran, *Les lettres d'el-Amarna* (1987).

The Stele of Merneptah:

W.M.F. Petrie, *Six Temples at Thebes* (1897), Pls. xiii–xiv.

P. Lacau, *Steles du nouvel empire,* I (1909), pp. 52–59, Pls. xvii–xix.

M. Lichtheim, *Ancient Egyptian Literature. A Book of Readings,* vol. 2 (1976), 73–78.

The Story of Aqhat:

C. Virolleaud, *La légende phenicienne de Daniel* (1936).

J. Obermann, *How Daniel Was Blessed with a Son* (1946).

M.D. Coogan, *Stories from Ancient Canaan* (1978), 27–47.

J.C. De Moor and K. Spronk, *A Cuneiform Anthology of Religious Texts from Ugarit* (1987), 102–121.

J.C. De Moor, *An Anthology of Religious Texts from Ugarit* (1987), 224–269.

The Diary of Wen Amon:

G. Moller, *Hieratische Lesestucke,* II (1927), 29.

A.H. Gardiner, *Late-Egyptian Stories* (1932), 61–76.

H. Goedicke, *The Report of Wenamun* (1975).

The Gezer Almanac:

W.F. Albright, "The Gezer Calendar," *BASOR* 82 (1943):18–24.

S. Talmon, "The Gezer Calendar and the Seasonal Cycle of Ancient Canaan," *JAOS* 83 (1963): 177–87.

J.C.L. Gibson, *Textbook of Syrian Semitic Inscriptions, I* (1971), 1–4.

The Mari Prophecies:

Archives Royales de Mari, Textes cuneiformes (quoted by number and volume).

F. Ellermeier, *Prophetie in Mari und Israel* (1968).

H.B. Huffmon, "Prophecy in the Mari Letters," *BA* 31/4 (1968), 101–124.

W.L. Moran, "New Evidence from Mari on the History of Prophecy," *Biblica* 50 (1969), 15–56.

The Stele of Mesha:

R. Dussaud, *Les monuments palestiniens et judaiques* (1912), 4–22.

J.C.L. Gibson, *Textbook of Syrian Semitic Inscriptions, I* (1971), 71–84.

The Karatepe Inscription:

H.T. Bossert and U.B. Alkim, *Karatepe* II (1947), Pls. xxix–xxxi, xl–xliv.

R.T. O'Callaghan, "The Phoenician Inscription on the King's Statue at Karatepe," *CBQ* 11 (1949), 233–48.

H.T. Bossert, et al., *Die Ausgrabungen auf dem Karatepe* (1950), Pl. xiv.

J. Pedersen, "The Phoenician Inscription of Karatepe," *Acta Orientalia* 21 (1953), 33–56.

The Annals of Shalmaneser III:

A.H. Layard, *Inscriptions in the Cuneiform Character* (1851).

The Black Obelisk of Shalmaneser III:

A.H. Layard, *Monuments of Nineveh* I (1849), Pls. 53–56.

———, *Inscriptions in the Cuneiform Character from Assyrian Monuments* (1851), Pls. 87–98.

The Annals of Tiglath-Pileser III:

P. Rost, *Die Keilschrifttexte Tiglat-Pilesers III nach den Papierabklatschen und Originalen des Britischen Museum* (1893).

The Annals of Sargon II:

H. Winckler, *Die Keilschrifttexte Sargons* (1889), Pl. 38.

R. Borger, *Babylonisch-Assyrische Lesestucke* (1963), 54–58.

The Siloam Inscription:

J.C.L. Gibson, *Textbook of Syrian Semitic Inscriptions, I* (1971), 21–23.

The Yavne-Yam Inscription:
J. Naveh, "A Hebrew Letter from the seventh century B.C.," *IEJ* 10 (1960): 129–39.
J.C.L. Gibson, *Textbook of Syrian Semitic Inscriptions, I* (1971), 26–30.

The Lachish Letters:
H. Torczyner, *Lachish I. The Lachish Letters* (1938), 33–43.
A. Lemaire, *Inscriptions hebraiques, I: Les ostraca* (1977), 97–100.
D. Pardee, *Handbook of Ancient Hebrew Letters* (1982), 78–81.

The Arad Letters:
J.C.L. Gibson, *Textbook of Syrian Semitic Inscriptions, I* (1971), 49–54.

The Annals of Sennacherib:
D.D. Luckenbill, *The Annals of Sennacherib* (1924).
R. Borger, *Babylonisch-assyrische Lesestucke* (1963), 67–69.

The Annals of Nebuchadnezzar:
D.J. Wiseman, *Chronicles of Chaldean Kings (626–556 B.C.) in the British Museum* (1956), 32–37, 73.

The Cylinder of Cyrus:
F.H. Weissbach, *Die Keilinschriften der Achameniden* (1911), 2–9.

The Hymn to the Aton:
N. de G. Davies, *The Rock Tombs of El-Amarna*, VI (1908), Pl. xxvii.

The Story of Ba'al and Anat:
C.H. Gordon, *Ugaritic Literature* (1949), 9–56.
M.D. Coogan, *Stories from Ancient Canaan* (1978), 75–115.
J.C. De Moor and K. Spronk, *A Cuneiform Anthology of Religious Texts from Ugarit* (1987), 1–44.
J.C. De Moor, *An Anthology of Religious Texts from Ugarit* (1987), 20–109.

The Lament for Ur:
S.N. Kramer, *The Lament Over the Destruction of Ur* (1940).
I. Bernhardt, *Sumerische literarische Texte aus Nippur II* (1967), 16, tablets 18–25.

The Story of Ahiqar:
T. Noldeke, *Untersuchungen zum Achiqar-Roman* (1914).
F. Stummer, *Der Kritische Wert der altaramaischen Ahikartexte aus Elephantine* (1914).
J.M. Lindenberger, *The Aramaic Proverbs of Ahiqar* (1983).

The Teachings of Ptah-Hotep:
G. Jequier, *Le Papyrus Prisse et ses variantes* (1911).
E. Devaud, *Les maximes de Ptah-hotep* (1916).
Z. Zaba, *Les Maximes de Ptahhotep* (1956).
M. Lichtheim, *Ancient Egyptian Literature. A Book of Readings,* vol. 1 (1975), 61–80.

The Teachings of Amenemope:
E.A.W. Budge, *Facsimiles of Egyptian Hieratic Papyri in the British Museum,* Second Series (1923), Pls. i–xiv.
———, *The Teachings of Amen-em-apt, Son of Kanakht* (1924).
I. Grumach, *Untersuchungen zur Lebenslehre des Amenope* (1972).
M. Lichtheim, *Ancient Egyptian Literature. A Book of Readings,* vol. 2 (1976), 146–63.

The Story of Keret:
H.L. Ginsberg, *The Legend of King Keret* (1946).
M.D. Coogan, *Stories from Ancient Canaan* (1978), 52–74.
J.C. De Moor and K. Spronk, *A Cuneiform Anthology of Religious Texts from Ugarit* (1987), 78–101.
J.C. De Moor, *An Anthology of Religious Texts from Ugarit* (1987), 191–223.

The Sufferer and the Soul:
A. Erman, *Gesprach eines Lebensmuden mit seiner Seele* (1896).
K. Sethe, *Aegyptische Lesestucke* (2nd ed., 1928), 43–46.
W. Barta, *Das Gesprach eines Mannes mit seinem Ba* (1969).
H. Goedicke, *The Report about the Dispute of a Man with His Ba* (1970).
M. Lichtheim, *Ancient Egyptian Literature. A Book of Readings,* vol. 1 (1975), 163–169.

The Farmer and The Courts:
F. Vogelsang and A.H. Gardiner, *Die Klagen des Bauern* (1908).
M. Lichtheim, *Ancient Egyptian Literature. A Book of Readings,* vol. 1 (1975), 169–184.

The Sufferer and The Friend:

J.A. Craig, *Babylonian and Assyrian Religious Texts,* I (1895), Pls. 44–52.

W.G. Lambert, *Babylonian Wisdom Literature* (1960), 63–91.

Egyptian Love Songs:

E.A.W. Budge, *Facsimiles of Egyptian Hieratic Papyri in the British Museum,* Second Series (1923), Pl. xliii.

M.V. Fox, *The Song of Songs and the Ancient Egyptian Love Songs* (1985).

The Visions of Neferti:

W. Golenischeff, *Les papyrus hieratiques no. 1115, 1116A, et 1116B de l'Ermitage Imperial à St. Petersbourg* (1913), Pls. 23–25.

M. Lichtheim, *Ancient Egyptian Literature. A Book of Readings,* vol. 1 (1975), 139–145.

H. Goedicke, *The Protocol of Neferyt* (1977).

Parallels Chart

Column 4 (*parallel*) in this chart uses a number and a key word to identify six ways in which the ancient Near Eastern texts, identified in column 3 (*text*) and located in column 2 (*page*), parallel the biblical texts listed in column 1 (*citation*). The parallels are based on:

1 = genre, e.g. creation story, flood story, law, teaching
2 = vocabulary, e.g. direct or similar words or phrases
3 = motif, e.g. barren wife, greed, widows & orphans, divine war
4 = social institution, e.g. anthropomorphism, taboo, propaganda
5 = plot, e.g. similar action in both texts
6 = historical event, e.g. person, place, event

CITATION	PAGE	TEXT	PARALLEL
GENESIS			
1:1–2:4a	86	Aqhat	5-seven day ritual
1:1–2	8	Enuma	1-creation story
			2-Tehom
1:2	29	Serpent	1-creation story
			5-chaos
1:3	33	Memphis	2-naming
1:6–7	13	Enuma	2-firmament
1:15–6	13	Enuma	2-moon
1:20–1	29	Serpent	1-creation story
			2-living beings
			3-fiat creation
1:22	29	Serpent	2-multitude
1:26–7	14	Enuma	2-humans
1:31–2:2	34	Memphis	2-rest
2:6–7	30	Serpent	1-creation story
			2-moisture/man

CITATION	PAGE	TEXT	PARALLEL
2:7	155	Aton	2-breathe
	20	Atrahasis	1-creation story
			4-anthropomorphism
	93	Aqhat	2-breathe
2:7-15	14	Enuma	5-humans
			4-anthropomorphism
4:1-26	41	Anubis	3-sibling rivalry
6:11-21	36	Gilgamesh	5-ark
6:14	24	Atrahasis	2-pitch
6:14-6	36	Gilgamesh	2-pitch
7:2-4, 7-9	37	Gilgamesh	5-animals
7:11	92	Aqhat	2-flood story
7:11-2, 17-23	37	Gilgamesh	2-darkness
7:13-6	37	Gilgamesh	5-hatch
7:24-8:3	38	Gilgamesh	5-aftermath
8:4	38	Gilgamesh	5-landing
8:5-17	38	Gilgamesh	5-release
8:20	38	Gilgamesh	5-sacrifice
8:21	26	Atrahasis	2-smell
8:21-22	39	Gilgamesh	3-remorse
9:1-17	40	Gilgamesh	5-hero's fate
9:12-7	39	Gilgamesh	1-covenant
			5-rainbow
9:20-3	87	Aqhat	2-drunk
10:9	89	Aqhat	2-hunter
14:19	117	Karatepe	1-blessing
			2-creator
15:1-4	85	Aqhat	3-barren wife
15:11	92	Aqhat	5-vultures
16:1-15	64	CH	3-heir
			4-surrogate
	85	Aqhat	3-barren wife
17:17	87	Aqhat	2-laughter
18:2	89	Aqhat	1-formula opening
			2-see in distance
18:6-7	89	Aqhat	5-meal
			4-hospitality
18:9-15	85	Aqhat	3-barren wife
19:1	89	Aqhat	2-gate
			3-testing
			4-place of justice
21:9-21	64	CH	3-heir
			4-surrogate
	86	Aqhat	1-heroic epic
			3-contest with god

CITATION	PAGE	TEXT	PARALLEL
21:20–1	89	Aqhat	2-hunter
25:21	85	Aqhat	5-pray for child
25:27	222	Friend	3-older vs. younger
27:38	93	Aqhat	1-blessing
			2-blessing
28:10–22	202	Keret	1-dream theophany
			5-dream
30:1–24	85	Aqhat	3-barren wife
30:40–2	42	Anubis	5-breeding
31:45–50	53	Treaty	1-covenant
			2-"If you"
			3-curse
31:51–3	53	Treaty	1-covenant
			2-gods witness
34	69	Sumerian	5-rape
35:17	21	Atrahasis	2-midwife
			3-birthing
38	71	Hittite	5-levir
	165	Ba'al	1-law (levir)
			3-heir
38:34	92	Aqhat	5-tear robe
			4-mourning ritual
39:7	43	Anubis	5-seduction
39:12	43	Anubis	5-seduction
39:17–9	44	Anubis	5-deception
41:34–6, 47–9	115	Karatepe	5-planning
			4-propaganda
EXODUS			
1:16	20	Atrahasis	2-birthstool
1:22–2:10	55	Sargon	5-reed boat
			3-miracle survival
3:14	28	Serpent	1-proclamation
			2-"I Am"
6:3	60	Balaam	2-Shaddai
19:10	159	Ba'al	5-washing
			4-ritual cleansing
20:12	182	Ahiqar	1-law
			2-honor parents
20:15	63	CH	2-theft
20:16	216	Farmer	1-law
			2-false witness
21:2–11	64	CH	2-slavery
21:15	66	CH	2-strike parents
21:16	63	CH	2-kidnapping

CITATION	PAGE	TEXT	PARALLEL
21:22–3	63	CH	2-miscarriage
21:23–5	67	CH	2-talion
21:28–36	67	CH	2-goring ox
22:2–3	63	CH	2-burglary
22:7–8	64	CH	2-stolen goods
22:16	69	Sumerian	2-seduce virgin
22:18	73	MAL	2-sorcery
22:26–7	133	Yavne-Yam	1-law
			2-pledge garment
	182	Ahiqar	1-law
			2-pledge garment
23:1–3	62	CH	2-false witness
30:23–33	61	Balaam	2-myrrh
			4-anointing ritual

LEVITICUS

18:6–18	65	CH	2-incest
			1-decalogue
	71	Hittite	4-marriage customs
19:11, 13	63	CH	2-theft
20:10–21	65	CH	3-illicit sex
20:13	73	MAL	2-homosexuality
20:27	73	MAL	2-sorcery
24:19–20	67	CH	2-talion

NUMBERS

5:11–31	64	CH	2-adultery
			4-ordeal
22:28–30	44	Anubis	1-fable
			5-talking animal
33:52	116	Karatepe	2-molten image

DEUTERONOMY

5:19	63	CH	2-theft
6:4–8	198	Amenemope	1-admonition
			2-fill
10:18	214	Farmer	1-law
			3-widows & orphans
15:12–8	64	CH	2-slavery
19:16–9	62	CH	2-false witness
19:21	67	CH	2-talion
21:1–9	93	Aqhat	4-forgiveness ritual
			5-burial

CITATION	PAGE	TEXT	PARALLEL
21:18–21	69	Sumerian	2-prodigal son
	182	Ahiqar	1-curse
			2-honor parents
22:1–4	63	CH	2-property
			4-social response
22:22	64	CH	2-adultery
22:23–4	69	Sumerian	2-raped virgin
			4-gate/justice place
22:23–7	64	CH	2-raped virgin
			4-justice of place
24:7	63	CH	2-kidnapping
25:5–10	71	Hittite	1-law (will)
			2-levir
	165	Ba'al	1-law (levir)
25:11–2	73	MAL	2-genitalia
			4-female taboo
27:20, 22–3	65	CH	2-incest
32:35	182	Ahiqar	1-law
			2-pledge garment

JOSHUA

2:6	105	Gezer	2-flax
6	203	Keret	5-seven day siege
6:17–21	113	Mesha	3-divine war
			5-herem
6:24	113	Mesha	3-divine
			5-herem
			3-divine war
6:26	93	Aqhat	1-curse
			2-rebuild
7:20–1	96	Wen-Amon	4-sacred property
8:1–17	113	Mesha	1-exhortation
			3-divine war
8:24–7	113	Mesha	3-divine
			5-herem
10:1–28	120	Shalmaneser	1-annal
			3-divine war
			5-alliance
10:42	113	Mesha	2-king
			3-divine war
11:1–12	120	Shalmaneser	1-annal
			3-divine war
			5-alliance

CITATION	PAGE	TEXT	PARALLEL
11:6–9	121	Shalmaneser	1-annal
			5-loot
19:8	137	Arad	6-Ramoth-negeb
JUDGES			
4:5	89	Aqhat	2-tree/justice
	88		4-justice site
4:17–22	93	Aqhat	3-revenge
			5-murder
4:19	93	Aqhat	4-hospitality
			5-drink request
5:27	164	Ba'al	5-victim falls
7:12	158	Ba'al	2-locusts
9:8–15	182	Ahiqar	1-fable
			5-taunt
11:30–1	203	Keret	1-oath
13:2–3	85	Aqhat	3-barren wife
16:3	168	Ba'al	4-power removed
			5-gate posts
19:22	116	Karatepe	2-trouble makers
21:25	238	Neferti	2-selfishness
			3-anarchy
RUTH			
2:2–9	197	Amenemope	1-law
			3-widows & orphans
			5-widow gleaning
2:23	105	Gezer	2-harvest
3:3	231	Love	2-anoint hair
4	71	Hittite	1-law
			5-levir
	165	Ba'al	1-law (levir)
4:1	89	Aqhat	2-gate
			4-site of justice
1 SAMUEL			
1:2–17	85	Aqhat	3-barren wife
1:21	116	Karatepe	2-sacrifice
3:3–4	23	Atrahasis	1-theophany
			5-dream
4:20	21	Atrahasis	2-midwife
6:13	105	Gezer	2-reaping
9:11	60	Balaam	2-seer
10:6	110	Mari	1-prophecy
			2-possession

CITATION	PAGE	TEXT	PARALLEL
12:14–5	110	Mari	1-admonition 2-king's duty 3-obedience to god
14:24	203	Keret	1-oath
15:1–6	201	Keret	5-son revolts
16:14–8	102	Wen-Amon	5-music
17:8–10	11	Enuma	1-taunt 5-single combat
18:7	167	Ba'al	1-song of praise
21:14	197	Amenemope	2-insanity 4-mental taboo
24:4	166	Ba'al	1-legal petition 4-hem = identity
24:5	110	Mari	2-hem 4-identity
26:19	132	Yavne-Yam	1-scribal address
28:3	73	MAL	5-witch
30:27	137	Arad	6-Ramoth-negeb
2 SAMUEL			
1:21	92	Aqhat	2-drought
2:18–23	12	Enuma	1-taunt 5-single combat
5:6–8	11	Enuma	1-taunt
5:8	11	Enuma	1-taunt
7:1–17	159	Ba'al	4-propaganda 5-house for god
7:13	163	Ba'al	1-covenant 4-divine right rule
8:2	12	Enuma	5-foot on foe
10:6–8	120	Shalmaneser	1-annal 5-alliance
12:15–7	93	Aqhat	5-seven day ritual
13:4–6	229	Love	5-fake illness
14:1–20	171	Lament	1-law 3-widows & orphans
15:1–6	205	Keret	5-son's revolt
15:2	88	Aqhat	2-gate 4-place of justice
15:3–5	110	Mari	1-admonition 4-king and law
15:4	215	Farmer	1-law 2-petitioners
15:14	205	Keret	5-king's flight

CITATION	PAGE	TEXT	PARALLEL
1 KINGS			
2:9	159	Ba'al	2-grey head
3:4–15	201	Keret	1-dream theophany
5:3–6	159	Ba'al	5-house for god
5:10–1	101	Wen-Amon	5-cedars cut
			6-cedars
9:15–20	116	Karatepe	1-annal
			4-propaganda
			5-fortresses
12:4	148	Cyrus	2-forced labor
			4-social unrest
13:2	239	Neferti	1-prophecy
			5-southern king
16:23–24	113	Mesha	6-Omri/Samaria
17:12–6	197	Amenemope	2-oil
			4-hospitality
18:36–45	164	Ba'al	5-god brings rain
18:42	162	Ba'al	3-subjection
			5-face in knees
19:19	105	Gezer	2-plowing
20:1–2	11	Enuma	1-taunt
21:1–4	213	Farmer	2-idols
			4-use of idols/gain
22:10	89	Aqhat	2-threshing floor
			4-place of justice
2 KINGS			
3:15	97	Wen-Amon	1-prophecy
			5-ecstatic
	110	Mari	1-prophecy
			5-ecstatic
3:20	137	Arad	6-"Way of Edom"
4:8–17	85	Aqhat	3-barren wife
4:34–7	204	Keret	1-miracle story
			5-cure
5:10–4	204	Keret	1-miracle story
			5-cure
9:1–10:33	124	Obelisk	6-Jehu
9:16–26	52	Treaty	1-covenant
			2-chariots
			4-reciprocity
9:36	45	Anubis	1-curse
			5-dogs eat corpse
14:9	182	Ahiqar	1-fable
			5-taunt

CITATION	PAGE	TEXT	PARALLEL
15:17–22	126	Tiglath-Pileser	6-tribute
17:3–6	128	Sargon II	6-fall of Samaria
17:24	116	Karatepe	5-deportation
18–19	139	Sennacherib	6-siege
18:13–37	95	Wen-Amon	1-threat
18:19–37	11	Enuma	1-taunt
20:20	131	Siloam	6-tunnel
24:1–17	142	Nebuchadnezzar	6-siege/fall
24:10	143	Nebuchadnezzar	6-siege
24:13–16	143	Nebuchadnezzar	6-loot
24:17	143	Nebuchadnezzar	6-new king

1 CHRONICLES

17:1–14	159	Ba'al	5-house for god

2 CHRONICLES

32:30	131	Siloam	6-tunnel

EZRA

1:1–4	147	Cyrus	6-temple funds
6:1–15	147	Cyrus	6-temple
6:3–5	147	Cyrus	6-temple
6:15	142	Nebuchadnezzar	2-month

NEHEMIAH

1:1	142	Nebuchadnezzar	2-month
8:18	86	Aqhat	5-seven day ritual

ESTHER

2:12	231	Love	2-anoint hair
3:7	142	Nebuchadnezzar	2-month

JOB

1:13–9	201	Keret	5-death of family
1:20	92	Aqhat	4-mourning ritual 5-tearing robe
3:17–9	207	Soul	2-death's release
5:26	218	Farmer	1-analogy 3-stages of life
7:1–10	218	Farmer	1-analogy 3-stages of life
7:13–4	171	Lament	2-bed's comforts
8:5–7	222	Friend	2-good to come
10:9	165	Ba'al	2-dust of grave

CITATION	PAGE	TEXT	PARALLEL
10:20–2	217	Eloquent	2-afterlife
			4-concept of death
11:7	222	Friend	2-depths of god
14:7–14	217	Farmer	2-afterlife
			4-concept of death
15:2–4	222	Friend	2-unwise words
15:5	223	Friend	2-lying mouth
18:5–21	221	Friend	2-wicked perish
20:20	217	Farmer	2-eyes
21:2–3	222	Friend	1-address mode
21:7–16	221	Friend	2-wicked prosper
24:12	217	Farmer	2-refuse to hear
38:16	160	Ba'al	2-springs of sea
39:5–8	182	Ahiqar	2-wild ass
42:1–6	165	Ba'al	3-submission
			5-hero surrenders
42:10–5	204	Keret	5-new family
PSALMS			
1	192	Amenemope	1-teaching
			2-tree
8:1	155	Aton	1-hymn of praise
			2-how majestic
8:2	181	Ahiqar	2-child
			3-unexpected wisdom
11:2	181	Ahiqar	2-shoot bow
16:9	158	Ba'al	2-glad heart
22:22–6	215	Farmer	1-hymn of praise
24:9	162	Ba'al	1-exhortation
			2-lift up heads
25:17	215	Farmer	1-legal petition
29:10	160	Ba'al	2-source of flood
31:15	196	Amenemope	3-worry
39:6	193	Amenemope	3-greed
41:13	169	Lament	1-doxology
42:1	165	Ba'al	2-spring/deer
49:5	193	Amenemope	3-greed
49:14	165	Ba'al	2-lure of death
52:2	180	Ahiqar	2-sharp words
52:7	193	Amenemope	3-greed
62:10	193	Amenemope	2-riches
			3-greed
	182	Ahiqar	3-greed
64:2–7	181	Ahiqar	2-shoot bow

CITATION	PAGE	TEXT	PARALLEL
68:4	159	Ba'al	2-cloud rider
	92	Aqhat	2-cloud rider
72:17	117	Karatepe	1-blessing
			2-name endures
74:13–4	11	Enuma	2-dragon
95:3	161	Ba'al	2-god is king
			3-divine king
96:4	161	Ba'al	2-god is king
			3-divine king
97:9	161	Ba'al	2-god is king
			3-divine king
101:8	116	Karatepe	2-destroy wicked
			4-civil order
103:14	197	Amenemope	1-creation story
			2-clay shapes
			4-anthropomorphism
104:3	159	Ba'al	2-cloud rider
	92	Aqhat	2-cloud rider
104:11–4	155	Aton	2-birds
104:20–1	154	Aton	2-darkness
104:22–3	154	Aton	2-daily schedule
104:24	155	Aton	2-sole power
104:25–6	155	Aton	2-sea
104:27	155	Aton	2-seasons
104:29–30	156	Aton	2-reliance on god
124:1–5	167	Ba'al	1-litany
			2-"If not"
125:3	168	Ba'al	2-broken scepter
126:4	167	Ba'al	2-wadis
129:3	167	Ba'al	2-plowing
			3-affliction image
131:1	181	Ahiqar	2-covet
132:7	166	Ba'al	2-footstool
132:18	167	Ba'al	2-shame
139:13	155	Aton	2-fertility
141:7	165	Ba'al	2-mouth of death
145:13	163	Ba'al	2-eternal kingdom
PROVERBS			
1:8	184	Ptah-Hotep	4-title of teacher
1:12	165	Ba'al	2-death swallows
1:17	184	Ptah-Hotep	1-saying form
2:1–5	185	Ptah-Hotep	1-address form
			2-seek wisdom

CITATION	PAGE	TEXT	PARALLEL
2:4	184	Ptah-Hotep	2-good advice
6:1–5	181	Ahiqar	2-pay debt
6:2	194	Amenemope	2-lies
6:16–9	179	Ahiqar	2-x/x + 1
			3-number progression
6:23–6	187	Ptah-Hotep	2-lust
6:24	184	Ptah-Hotep	2-women
6:27–9	187	Ptah-Hotep	2-lust
7:24–7	187	Ptah-Hotep	2-lust
9:1	161	Ba'al	2-seven pillars
9:17	184	Ptah-Hotep	1-analogy
10:1	184	Ptah-Hotep	1-analogy
11:21	185	Ptah-Hotep	2-justice
12:4	188	Ptah-Hotep	2-good wife
13:24	179	Ahiqar	2-discipline
14:5	195	Amenemope	2-false witness
15:16	193	Amenemope	1-"Better" proverb
			3-be satisfied
15:17	193	Amenemope	1-"Better" proverb
			3-be satisfied
16:8	193	Amenemope	2-god's majesty
16:9	196	Amenemope	1-"Better" proverb
			3-be satisfied
15:27	187	Ptah-Hotep	2-greed
17:1	196	Amenemope	1-"Better" proverb
			2-eating
			3-be satisfied
17:5	197	Amenemope	2-laugh/stricken
17:13	185	Ptah-Hotep	2-evil
19:1, 22	193	Amenemope	1-"Better" proverb
			3-be satisfied
19:18	179	Ahiqar	2-discipline
19:21	196	Amenemope	2-god's majesty
20:4	104	Gezer	2-planting
20:9	196	Amenemope	2-hypocrisy
20:20	182	Ahiqar	2-honor parents
21:6	193	Amenemope	2-riches
22:17–8	190	Amenemope	1-admonition
			2-heart
22:20	198	Amenemope	1-admonition
			2-study
22:20–1	190	Amenemope	2-thirty
22:22	191	Amenemope	2-rob poor
22:24	194	Amenemope	2-fool

CITATION	PAGE	TEXT	PARALLEL
22:25	194	Amenemope	2-bad company
22:26–7	195	Amenemope	1-admonition
			2-forgive debt
22:28	192	Amenemope	2-landmark
			4-property taboo
22:29	198	Amenemope	2-skill
23:1	184	Ptah-Hotep	2-table manners
23:1–3	185	Ptah-Hotep	2-table manners
23:4	193	Amenemope	2-strive/greed
23:5	194	Amenemope	2-riches/wings
23:6–7	194	Amenemope	2-false oaths
23:8	195	Amenemope	2-vomit
			3-waste
23:10	192	Amenemope	2-landmark
			4-property taboo
23:11	192	Amenemope	2-please ruler
			4-property taboo
25:11	184	Ptah-Hotep	1-analogy
25:13	186	Ptah-Hotep	2-reliability
25:15b	181	Ahiqar	2-king's tongue
25:21–2	191	Amenemope	2-feed hungry
26:2	180	Ahiqar	2-word
26:7	184	Ptah-Hotep	1-analogy
27:1	196	Amenemope	2-worry
27:3	181	Ahiqar	2-debt
29:13	197	Amenemope	2-poor & rich
			3-fate
29:14–6	205	Keret	1-law
			3-widows & orphans
31:10–1 + 27–31	188	Ptah-Hotep	2-good wife

ECCLESIASTES

3:1–10	197	Amenemope	2-time
			3-fate
3:3	10	Enuma	2-power
3:12	193	Amenemope	2-be content
3:16		Dialogue	2-inconsistencies
			3-anarchy
3:20	165	Ba'al	2-dust of grave
5:2	180	Ahiqar	2-word
5:10	193	Amenemope	2-strive/greed
6:2–3	188	Ptah-Hotep	2-wealth
6:10	180	Ahiqar	2-obey authority
9:7	179	Ahiqar	2-wine

CITATION	PAGE	TEXT	PARALLEL
10:9	181	Ahiqar	2-woodcutter
			3-reversal
11:2	161	Ba'al	2-x/x +1
			3-number progression
CANTICLES			
2:5	230	Love	5-love sick
2:10-3	229	Love	5-fertile land
4:10	229	Love	2-love/wine
5:1	229	Love	2-intoxication
5:2-6	230	Love	2-door/latch
			3-double entendre
5:8	229	Love	5-love sick
7:5	228	Love	2-hair snare
			3-trap
7:13	229	Love	2-mandrake
7:13-4	228	Love	2-mandrake
			3-love garden
ISAIAH			
5:6	105	Gezer	2-pruning vines
5:8-23	175	Lament	1-prophecy
			2-Woe!
5:14	165	Ba'al	2-death's mouth
6:10	217	Farmer	2-see/not see
9:3	105	Gezer	2-harvest
10:2	205	Keret	1-law
			3-widows & orphans
10:6	91	Aqhat	2-trample
10:15	180	Ahiqar	2-obey authority
18:5	105	Gezer	2-pruning vines
22:21	115	Karatepe	2-father
29:16	197	Amenemope	1-creation story
			2-potter's clay
			4-anthropomorphism
45:1	147	Cyrus	4-propaganda
			5-chosen king
45:6	115	Karatepe	1-realm formula
			2-rising sun
			4-universal rule
45:9	197	Amenemope	1-creation story
			2-potter's clay
			4-anthropomorphism
	180	Ahiqar	2-obey authority

CITATION	PAGE	TEXT	PARALLEL
46:4	160	Ba'al	2-grey hair
51:17–8	87	Aqhat	5-solace a drunk
63:3–6	158	Ba'al	3-divine war
			5-wading in blood
64:9	197	Amenemope	1-creation story
			2-potter's clay
			4-anthropomorphism
JEREMIAH			
1:10	10	Enuma	1-investiture
			2-power
7:2–4	45	Anubis	1-law
			4-oath before god
			5-argue case
7:33	121	Shalmaneser	5-unburied bodies
9:4–5	210	Soul	2-neighbor
			3-anarchy
9:21–2	174	Lament	5-dead in squares
11:5	167	Ba'al	2-land/honey
11:6	192	Amenemope	2-tree
11:19	175	Lament	2-lamb/slaughter
	159	Ba'al	2-lamb/slaughter
12:1	221	Friend	2-wicked prosper
13:23	183	Ahiqar	2-professions
			3-order in life
15:7	170	Lament	2-gate
			4-site of justice
	167	Ba'al	2-winnowing
16:4	174	Lament	5-unburied bodies
16:6	165	Ba'al	4-destruction ritual
			5-mourning
17:5–8	192	Amenemope	2-tree
18:2–6	17	Atrahasis	1-creation story
			2-potter's clay
			4-anthropomorphism
21:4–5	181	Ahiqar	2-shoot bow
26:16–9	163	Ba'al	4-immune prophets
			5-immunity
26:20–2	135	Lachish	6-Elnathan
30:4–5	175	Lament	1-petition
31:38–40	175	Lament	1-petition
			2-restoration
34:1–7	147	Cyrus	6-Jerusalem
34:6–7	136	Lachish	6-Azekah/Lachish

CITATION	PAGE	TEXT	PARALLEL
37:1	142	Nebuchadnezzar	6-Zedekiah
40:10	105	Gezer	2-reaping fruit
51:2	167	Ba'al	2-winnowing
			4-divine justice
51:59	138	Arad	6-invasion of Judah

LAMENTATIONS

2:10	61	Balaam	2-garment
			3-reversal
			4-mourning ritual
3:2	60	Balaam	2-darkness
4:3–4	174	Lament	2-daughter
			3-anarchy
4:5	173	Lament	5-dead revelers

EZEKIEL

8:14	157	Ba'al	4-mourning ritual
9:4	237	Neferti	2-regret
17:5	192	Amenemope	2-tree
22:7	205	Keret	1-law
			3-widows & orphans
27:30	165	Ba'al	4-destruction ritual
			5-mourning
37	175	Lament	1-prophecy
			3-restoration
37:1–2	121	Shalmaneser	2-battlefield
37:9	93	Aqhat	2-breath of life

DANIEL

4:6	235	Neferti	5-wise men
9:16–9	236	Neferti	1-plea
			2-restoration
11:2–4	239	Neferti	2-divided land
11:14	238	Neferti	2-take up arms
11:20–4	239	Neferti	2-weak rulers
12:1	240	Neferti	5-triumphant king

HOSEA

6:2	179	Ahiqar	2-x/x + 1
			3-number progression
5:19	192	Amenemope	2-landmark
10:4	216	Farmer	2-truth
11:1	109	Mari	2-"raised you"
			3-father/son
13:14–5	164	Ba'al	2-drying winds
14:9	198	Amenemope	1-admonition
			2-guidance

CITATION	PAGE	TEXT	PARALLEL
JOEL			
2:10	60	Balaam	2-darkness
AMOS			
2:6–7	205	Keret	1-law
			2-hear poor
2:7	223	Friend	2-trample needy
2:8	133	Yavne-Yam	1-law
			2-garment/pledge
4:3	173	Lament	2-breached wall
5:10	223	Friend	2-honest quieted
5:10–3	216	Farmer	2-criminals
			3-anarchy
5:12	216	Farmer	1-law
			2-bribes
		Keret	2-failed justice
5:14	217	Farmer	2-evil for good
5:14–5	210	Soul	2-evil & good
			3-anarchy
5:15	109	Mari	1-admonition
			2-justice
5:16	175	Lament	1-lament
			2-"Alas!"
5:18–20	170	Lament	3-"Day of Lord"
8:1	105	Gezer	2-summer fruit
8:4–6	216	Farmer	2-false scales
MICAH			
4:9	38	Gilgamesh	2-travail
6:3	79	Amarna	1-petition
			2-what done?
6:8	220	Friend	3-humility
	216	Farmer	2-"do justice"
6:11	216	Farmer	2-false scales
6:12	216	Farmer	2-lying tongue
HABAKKUK			
3:17	165	Ba'al	2-produce dies
ZECHARIAH			
1:3	159	Ba'al	1-exhortation
			2-"return"
7:1	142	Nebuchadnezzar	2-month
12:1–9	170	Lament	2-"In that day"
			3-Day of the Lord

CITATION	PAGE	TEXT	PARALLEL
MALACHI			
1:11	115	Karatepe	1-realm formula
			2-rising sun
			4-universal rule
JUDITH			
13:2, 6, 9	94	Aqhat	3-revenge
			5-murder
WISDOM OF SOLOMON			
1:15	212	Farmer	1-teaching
			2-justice
			3-eternal things
8:13	212	Farmer	1-teaching
			2-justice
			3-eternal things
10:21	181	Ahiqar	2-child
			3-unexpected wisdom
SIRACH			
6:7	184	Ptah-Hotep	2-friend
8:1	184	Ptah-Hotep	2-powerful man
9:1	184	Ptah-Hotep	2-wife
22:14–5	181	Ahiqar	2-debt
27:16	180	Ahiqar	2-word
28:17	181	Ahiqar	2-king's tongue
31:12	184	Ptah-Hotep	2-table manners
MATTHEW			
7:12	216	Farmer	1-teaching
			2-golden rule
16:19	10	Enuma	2-power to bind
18:27	195	Amenemope	1-admonition
			2-debt forgiven
21:16	181	Ahiqar	2-child
			3-unexpected wisdom
HEBREWS			
4:12	180	Ahiqar	2-ruler's words
JAMES			
3:1–18	188	Amenemope	2-hot heads

Abbreviations

Ahiqar	The Story of Ahiqar
Amarna	The El Amarna Letters
Amenemope	The Teachings of Amen-em-ope
Anubis	The Story of Anubis and Bata
Aqhat	The Story of Aqhat
Arad	The Arad Letters
Aton	The Hymn to the Aton
Atrahasis	The Atrahasis Story
Ba'al	The Story of Ba'al and Anat
Balaam	The Story of Balaam
CH	The Code of Hammurabi
Cyrus	The Cylinder of Cyrus
Enuma	The Enuma Elish Story
Farmer	The Farmer and The Courts
Friend	The Sufferer and The Friend
Gezer	The Gezer Almanac
Hittite	The Hittite Code
Karatepe	The Karatepe Inscription
Keret	The Story of Keret
Lachish	The Lachish Letters
Lament	The Lament for Ur
Love	Egyptian Love Songs
MAL	The Middle Assyrian Code
Mari	The Mari Prophecies
Memphis	The Memphis Creation Story
Mesha	The Stele of Mesha
Nebuchadnezzar	The Annals of Nebuchadnezzar
Neferti	The Visions of Neferti
Ptah-Hotep	The Teachings of Ptah-Hotep
Sargon	The Story of Sargon's Birth
Sargon II	The Annals of Sargon II
Sennacherib	The Annals of Sennacherib
Serpent	The Story of Ra and The Serpent